KINSHIP
and
MARRIAGE
in Genesis

KINSHIP
and
MARRIAGE
in Genesis

A Household
Economics Perspective

NAOMI STEINBERG

Fortress Press   Minneapolis

KINSHIP AND MARRIAGE IN GENESIS
A Household Economics Perspective

Scripture quotations from the Revised Standard Version of the Bible are copyright © 1946, 1952, 1971 by the Division of Christian Education of the National Council of Churches of Christ in the United States of America. Used by permission.

Portions of chapter one appeared in a different form as "Alliance or Descent? The Function of Marriage in Genesis" in *Journal for the Study of the Old Testament* 51 (1991) 45–55 and are reprinted by permission of Sheffield Academic Press. Portions of chapter two appeared in a different form as "The Genealogical Framework of the Family Stories in Genesis" in *Semeia* 46 (1989) 41–50 and are reprinted by permission of *Semeia*.

Cover design: Baker Group Design
Interior design: ediType

Library of Congress Cataloging-in-Publication Data

Steinberg, Naomi A.
    Kinship and marriage in Genesis : a household economics perspective / Naomi Steinberg.
        p. cm.
    Includes bibliographical references and indexes.
    ISBN 0-8006-2703-2 (alk. paper)
    1. Bible. O.T. Genesis XI, 10–L, 26—Criticism, interpretation, etc. 2. Family—Biblical teaching. I. Title.
BS1235.2.S755 1993
221'.1106—dc20   93-572
                                                                  CIP

The paper used in this publication meets the minimum requirements of American National Standard for Information Sciences—Permanence of Paper for Printed Library Materials, ANSI Z329.48-1984. ∞™

Manufactured in the U.S.A.   AF 1–2703

97   96   95   94   93   1   2   3   4   5   6   7   8   9   10

In memory of
my grandmothers, Sylvia and Bella,
who ensured the survival of my family tree through difficult times;
and my grandfathers, Jacob and Morris,
who were wise enough to marry them.

Contents

Preface

My interest in Genesis goes back to my 1984 Columbia University dissertation. Although the present work bears no resemblance to that earlier study, I want to take this opportunity to thank the three individuals who mentored me at that time: George M. Landes, Gillian Lindt, and Viviana Zelizer.

The idea for this book was born and nurtured during my time on the Religious Studies Faculty of DePaul University. With a Summer Research Grant from the College of Liberal Arts and Sciences, I laid the theoretical groundwork for this project in 1988. That research resulted in an article in *JSOT* 51 (1991). I owe thanks to my colleagues in Religious Studies for their generous encouragement of my interest in cross-cultural analysis of family life in the Bible.

The two individuals whose unwavering support and assistance have transcended the two stages of my research on Genesis are Thomas B. Dozeman and David L. Petersen. The latter put in many hours reading drafts of both the dissertation and this book; his thorough critiques have taught me much.

This book has also benefited from the careful readings and helpful comments of its two reviewers, Peggy L. Day and Jo Ann Hackett. I am grateful for their efforts on my behalf.

I owe a debt of gratitude for their editorial assistance to Marshall D. Johnson and Charles B. Puskas of Fortress Press. It is a pleasure to thank them for all their help. Thanks are also due to my colleague William VanderMarck for his careful proofreading

of the final manuscript. Finally, Robyn Carlson generously provided her computer expertise in designing the genealogical chart
in this book.

Last but not least I wish to remember the friend who years ago
remarked of my interest in Genesis, "Simple stories for simple
minds." By writing this book, I have tried to prove him wrong.

Abbreviations

AB	Anchor Bible
AOAT	Alter Orient und Altes Testament
ATANT	Abhandlungen zur Theologie des Alten und Neuen Testaments
BA	*Biblical Archaeologist*
BASOR	*Bulletin of the American Schools of Oriental Research*
BBB	Bonner biblische Beiträge
BR	*Biblical Research*
BWANT	Beiträge zur Wissenschaft vom Alten und Neuen Testament
BZ	*Biblische Zeitschrift*
BZAW	Beihefte zur *Zeitschrift für die alttestamentliche Wissenschaft*
CBQ	*Catholic Biblical Quarterly*
GKC	Gesenius's Hebrew Grammar, ed. E. Kautzsch, tr. A. E. Cowley
HUCA	*Hebrew Union College Annual*
Int	*Interpretation*
JAAR	*Journal of the American Academy of Religion*
JANESCU	*Journal of the Ancient Near Eastern Society of Columbia University*

JAOS	*Journal of the American Oriental Society*
JBL	*Journal of Biblical Literature*
JJS	*Journal of Jewish Studies*
JNES	*Journal of Near Eastern Studies*
JSOT	*Journal for the Study of the Old Testament*
JSOTSup	Journal for the Study of the Old Testament—Supplement Series
LXX	Septuagint
OTL	Old Testament Library
OTS	*Oudtestamentische Studiën*
RB	*Revue biblique*
RHR	*Revue de l'histoire des religions*
SBT	Studies in Biblical Theology
Sem	*Semitica*
ST	*Studia theologica*
VT	*Vetus Testamentum*
VTSup	Vetus Testamentum, Supplements
ZAW	*Zeitschrift für die alttestamentliche Wissenschaft*

Introduction

In this study I am concerned with the nature of kinship and marriage in the ancestral stories of Gen 11:10—50:26. I address this topic using the general methodology of social anthropology, a discipline concerned with social organization, and the subdiscipline of household economics, an approach that examines family units. The household economics approach sets the analysis of family life within the wider framework of comparative studies linking economics, production, and reproduction. It allows us to see that specific domestic arrangements in ancient Israel conform to social norms that further the social and economic development of the family. One of the goals of this study is to investigate the relationship between inheritance, descent, and marriage and, thereby, to assess the marriage choices made by the characters in the ancestral stories.

This analysis of the social dimensions of family life in Genesis distinguishes the present study from others in which literary concerns predominate. The analytical model that is developed in this work relies on comparative data from kinship studies as well as the methods of traditional Hebrew Bible scholarship. The results of this study make it possible to see the ancestral stories of Genesis in a new fashion. I will be asking the following questions: What conditions explain the occurrence of monogamy or polygyny in the social world of Genesis? How is inheritance divided among family members? How does the timing of the passing on of an inheritance affect marriage arrangements and the event of family fission? The comparative perspectives provided by social anthropology demonstrate that in the case of ancient Israel the answers to these questions differ from those that come from our own society.

Turning to literary-critical analysis, another goal of this study is to provide a fresh assessment of some contemporary issues in pentateuchal research. I argue that we reconsider M. Noth's analysis of the secondary character of the Genesis genealogies and recognize the interrelationship between narrative and genealogy. It seems clear that the genealogies are primary in Genesis.

Finally, although this study raises gender-related concerns, its methods and perspectives derive from social-scientific and literary issues. It does not intend to evaluate either women's or men's social position in ancient Israel in the light of contemporary evaluation of gender roles, or the so-called sexist nature of the Hebrew Bible. I concur with the argument that much recent discussion of issues of power inherent in the term *patriarchy* reflects modern concerns that some biblical scholars have inappropriately read back into ancient Israelite society, where they are not relevant.[1] However, despite the fact that this study is not a feminist reading of gender issues, it does reflect on "the syntax of social

---

1. For an excellent discussion of "the problem of patriarchy," see C. Meyers, *Discovering Eve* (New York: Oxford Univ. Press, 1988) 24–46. Meyers attempts to reconstruct the world of Israelite women using social-scientific analysis. She cautions that we must not read into the biblical texts issues relevant to contemporary women's experiences. By contrast, S. P. Jeansonne argues that feminist interests are relevant in the study of biblical texts and that patriarchal biases are inherent in the tradition (*The Women of Genesis* [Minneapolis: Fortress, 1990]). Although her study employs the methodology of literary criticism, her conclusions are grounded in ideological and psychological categories relevant to women in society today—but not necessarily appropriate for the women of ancient Israel. Her interest lies in elevating women and devaluing men. When it becomes impossible for her to present Israelite women as appropriate role models for women today, she shifts from analysis of individuals to etiological explanations. For example, when she takes up Sarah's expulsion of Hagar and Ishmael in Genesis 21, Jeansonne avoids the meaning of the strife between the two women by arguing that the women represent nations rather than individuals. The work of S. J. Teubal also argues that men's concerns have obscured women's lives in the Hebrew Bible. Her analysis is difficult to accept if the reader does not agree with her premise that Sarah had a role similar to that of a *nadītu* princess; see S. J. Teubal, *Sarah the Priestess: The First Matriarch of Genesis* (Athens, Ohio: Swallow, 1984); idem, *Hagar the Egyptian* (San Francisco: Harper & Row, 1990).

relationships"[2] and does not simply accept past analysis of family life. Consequently, I hope the results of this study will interest both the scholarly and the less technically trained reader. To that end, technical details, including discussion of topics pertinent to the Hebrew original of the text, have been kept to a minimum. These matters are analyzed in the footnotes. A glossary that defines select terms relevant to this work appears at the end of the text.

---

2. P. Culham, "Ten Years after Pomeroy: Studies of the Image and Reality of Women in Antiquity," *Rescuing Creusa: New Methodological Approaches to Women in Antiquity* (ed. M. Skinner; *Helios*, n.s. 13; Lubbock: Texas Tech Univ. Press, 1987) 10.

Chapter 1

Theoretical Considerations

The Function of Marriage: Kinship Issues

This study examines family organization in the Hebrew Bible from the perspective of the individual within the kinship system and maintains that the stories in Gen 11:10—50:26 are concerned with genealogical continuity and inheritance. I argue that the biblical narratives explore strategies in ancient Israelite society for establishing heirship and inheritance of property. Because life does not exist in the ideal and the opportunity to designate a biological heir is not always available, the texts present various problems that may interrupt the line of descent. In consequence, the stories investigate the various options for establishing heirship. The narratives make clear that a woman within the patrilineage of Terah is an appropriate potential spouse for a man in the Israelite line of inheritance. These endogamous marriages within the patrilineage begun by Terah constitute the Israelite descent line of Abraham.[1]

---

1. Leach reaches similar conclusions by means of a different route; see E. Leach, *Genesis as Myth and Other Essays* (London: Jonathan Cape, 1969) 7–23. Lemche notes that the lineage of Terah is the only one for which we have complete information. Speaking of general marriage practices in ancient Israel, he argues that while there was a preference for endogamy, numerous exceptions to this rule exist; see N. P. Lemche, *Early Israel* (VTSup 37; Leiden: E. J. Brill, 1985) 272–74. Recently, some have argued that the lineage of Terah descends through Abram, rather than either Nahor or Haran, because Abram is the one who was

Further, in the family stories marriage functions to establish descent[2] rather than to form alliances.[3] Kinship endogamy is traced through the collateral (sibling) patrilineage of Terah. From the vantage point of Israelite exclusivity, boundaries of endogamy are narrowly drawn. In addition, the linking relative in the genealogy is the male spouse. Throughout the ancient Near East, marriage functions to establish inheritance of land, but only patrilineal collateral marriage within the line of Terah establishes the right to claim the land of Israel.

Before we can interpret the implications of marriage decisions for the transmission of the lineage and its land, we must specify the level of society being examined because the function of marriage may change depending on whether one is considering familial succession or seeking to explain political relationships in the ancient world. Our understanding of how kinship affects decisions on the transmission of property is determined by whether we are analyzing relationships over time and space—seeking the interconnection of lineages as a whole—or are considering them from the perspective of the individual within the system. We cannot assume a priori knowledge of the appropriate boundaries for endogamy (in-marriage) and exogamy (out-marriage). Instead we must explore marriage patterns as they are presented in the texts. Although the data on kinship provided in the Bible are incomplete—not only is our understanding of the terminology imprecise, but we also lack information with regard to personal names and kinship relationships—enough data are available to establish the influences of specific kinship relationships for particular marriage choices.[4]

I intend to explore marriage relationships less from the external perspective, that of historical hindsight on sociopolitical issues, and more from the internal perspective, the unfolding of

circumcised; see T. J. Prewitt, *The Elusive Covenant* (Bloomington and Indianapolis: Indiana Univ. Press, 1990) 27–30; and H. Eilberg-Schwartz, *The Savage in Judaism* (Bloomington and Indianapolis: Indiana Univ. Press, 1990) 167.

2. M. Fortes, "The Structure of Unilineal Descent Groups," *American Anthropologist* 55 (1953) 17–41.

3. C. Lévi-Strauss, *The Elementary Structures of Kinship* (rev. ed.; Boston: Beacon, 1969); French original, 1949.

4. While descent is absolute and established through blood ties to a particular ancestor, kinship is relative and can be based on either blood or marriage connections to an individual.

social patterns within the society depicted in the text. For example, one should assume that when Abraham fathers a child through Hagar (Genesis 16), Ishmael is eligible at that stage in the family's history to function as direct heir to his father. One properly explains Isaac, rather than Ishmael, as the chosen heir (Gen 21:8-14) because of their respective mothers' statuses (the internal point of view)—rather than, improperly, by arguing that Ishmael married an Egyptian woman in order to form an alliance with his mother's people and that as a consequence of this alliance Ishmael was assigned land geographically adjacent to Israel (the external point of view; Gen 25:12-18).[5] Viewed from an internal perspective, the stories of Genesis provide information on "strategies of heirship."[6] Instead of arguing that Hagar's child cannot be Abraham's heir because his mother is of low status, we have to separate her status from that of Ishmael and assume her child is an acceptable heir to Abraham until such a time as a child is borne to Abraham by another woman who has stronger family rights than Hagar. Otherwise, it is improbable that the plan to obtain an heir through Hagar would have ever been proposed by Sarah and accepted by Abraham.

To be sure, both points of view are legitimate. They are, however, relevant to different levels of social analysis, the "family" versus the "nation." Although the kinship connections reinforced through marriage may be "fictional"—that is, created to justify political issues from an external perspective—one should assume such marriages to be sociologically correct, at least from the perspective of the ancient author. Certain marriages take priority over others in establishing how an individual becomes affiliated with the Israelite lineage.

---

5. The questions asked of the texts differ when we do not assume the sociopolitical results of Israelite history but are instead interested in what we are learning about marriage and inheritance from the stories as they unfold.

6. J. Goody, *Production and Reproduction* (Cambridge Studies in Social Anthropology 17; Cambridge: Cambridge Univ. Press, 1976) 86–98. More recently, Goody expresses a preference for the phrase "strategies of continuity"; see J. Goody, *The Orient, the Ancient and the Primitive: Systems of Marriage and the Family in the Preindustrial Societies of Eurasia* (Cambridge: Cambridge Univ. Press, 1990) 3. I wish to thank my colleague John Dominic Crossan for calling the latter book to my attention.

One Approach Influenced by Lévi-Strauss

One approach to the question of the function of marriage is attested in three recent works, all of which develop the thesis that marriages in Genesis are made for the purpose of forming alliances.[7] The authors of these three works rely to varying degrees on Lévi-Strauss's understanding of kinship structure. Building on his theories concerning wife-givers and wife-takers, they have understood marriages to be alliances. The ideal marriage is one based on an exchange of women between two groups who are neither too closely linked nor too distantly related. They deem the ideal union from the perspective of the groom is matrilateral, cross-cousin marriage (mother's brother's daughter). It is a marriage between two individuals who are already related across the generations but are not of the same clan or tribe.

However, by using Lévi-Strauss's work, those who argue that these marriages provide evidence of matrilateral, cross-cousin marriage in ancient Israel fail to note that preference for marriage to a mother's brother's daughter is a characteristic of matrilineal societies; alliance marriages based on the exchange of women are found in groups practicing exogamous marriages. In order to argue convincingly for the practice of alliance marriages in Genesis, the pool for the exchange of women must be wider than that described in the biblical texts because men are expected to "marry in a circle." Thus, when M. E. Donaldson quotes Robin Fox in support of her argument for the alliance basis of marriage ("Wife-givers cannot be wife-takers; a group cannot give women to a group from which it has taken women"),[8] she invokes a marriage rule that is not attested by the biblical data.

The sample provided in Genesis is not wide enough to indicate that men exchange women to form marriage alliances. For example, in order to sustain his argument for a circulating con-

7. M. E. Donaldson, "Kinship Theory in the Patriarchal Narratives: The Case of the Barren Wife," *JAAR* 49 (1981) 77–87; T. J. Prewitt, "Kinship Structures and the Genesis Genealogies," *JNES* 40 (1981) 87–98; R. A. Oden, "Jacob as Father, Husband, and Nephew: Kinship Studies and the Patriarchal Narratives," *JBL* 102 (1983) 189–205. Oden updates and expands his discussion of these issues in "The Patriarchal Narratives as Myth: The Case of Jacob," *The Bible without Theology: The Theological Tradition and Alternatives to It* (San Francisco: Harper & Row, 1987) 106–30, 183–87.

8. Donaldson, "Kinship Theory," 82; R. Fox, *Marriage and Kinship: An Anthropological Perspective* (Baltimore: Penguin, 1962) 208.

nubium, T. J. Prewitt must speculate that, to receive a wife, Lot accompanied Abraham when they left their homeland.[9] This alliance would complete the circle set up when Haran gave a woman to Nahor's line, and then Nahor's line gave women to Abraham's line; now Abraham must give a woman back to Haran's line. The data needed to maintain this argument are incomplete, requiring too high a degree of speculation on Prewitt's part. He has introduced an anthropological model that does not explain the Hebrew Bible data. It makes more sense to understand Lot's rationale for traveling with Abraham for purposes of inheritance; when a man has no lineal heir, one strategy available to him is to designate his brother's son as his heir.[10] Instead, Genesis emphasizes that the line of Abraham takes wives from the line of Nahor, not that the women are exchanged in a circulating connubium.

The Approach Used in This Study

The anthropological theory I use in this study distinguishes social structure from social organization and understands social organization regarding descent and inheritance to play a powerful role in the family stories in Genesis. As R. Firth has stated the matter:

> A structural principle is one which provides a fixed line of social behaviour and represents the order which it manifests. The concept of social organization has complementary emphasis. It recognizes adaptation of behaviour in respect of given ends, control of means in varying circumstances, which are set by changes in the external environment or by the necessity to resolve conflict between structural principles. If structure implies order, organization implies working towards order—though not necessarily in the same order.[11]

In other words, there is a distinction between how the world ought to work, the ideal, and how it actually does work, the reality. Thus, while the structural level emphasizes repetition of social relations within a particular situation, without concern for individual

---

9. Prewitt, "Kinship Structures"; see, more recently, Prewitt, *The Elusive Covenant*, 24–27.

10. Goody, *Production and Reproduction*, 75.

11. R. Firth, "Some Principles of Social Organization," *Essays in Social Organization and Values* (London School of Economics Monographs on Social Anthropology 28; London: Athlone, 1964) 61.

choice, the organizational level concerns itself with individual decisions made in adapting to external circumstances. The study of social organization recognizes individual flexibility in decision making, while, at the same time, it abstracts a "pattern-sequence," which reflects the implications of recurring individual choice. Alternative behaviors or strategies may all be aimed at achieving the same goal—but may also be occasioned by changes in the external environment. For example, in a situation where the issue of inheritance is crucial, both barrenness and sterility must be confronted, but they need not be the controlling concern. If a man does not have a biological heir, he may utilize different strategies in order to find a substitute heir. In order to be able to view the function of marriage from the organizational perspective, we must not separate synchronic behavior (marriage decisions) from diachronic behavior (descent decisions). The intersection of these two factors indicates clearly that a man's choice of a wife has implications for whether he becomes part of the Israelite descent line.

When describing descent relations in Genesis, we must draw the social boundaries for separating endogamy from exogamy. But from what perspective (internal or external) are these boundaries maintained and for what purposes?[12] In Genesis, we find a pattern in which a marriage is legitimate if it enables heirship. All the marriages described in Gen 11:10—50:26 are "legitimate" because they lead to offspring. Even the union between Lot and his two daughters, which leads to the birth of the Moabites and Ammonites (Gen 19:30-38), is legitimate in this sense. This latter case may not be part of the vertical Israelite lineage, but this fact does not diminish the narrative's function in establishing the claim to land in the ancient Near East.

The narratives concerning Jacob and Esau illustrate the manner in which kinship boundaries determine heirship. Either Jacob or Esau could be his father's heir, since both sons are biological sons of Isaac. In addition to having the correct father, Jacob and Esau have an appropriate mother to allow for heirship. The marriage of Isaac and Rebekah involves patrilineal endogamy because both individuals can trace patrilineage to Terah. Hence,

---

12. Oden, "Jacob as Father," 196; K. R. Andriolo, "A Structural Analysis of Genealogy and Worldview in the Old Testament," *American Anthropologist* 75 (1973) 1663.

one must ask: Why does only one son qualify to continue the Israelite lineage when the genealogical claim of having the correct father is maintained by the other son as well? Esau continues his father's lineage, but he is now outside the vertical Israelite lineage because he marries the "wrong" woman. Mahalath (Gen 28:9), who is a daughter of a son of Abraham, is external to the Israelite lineage. Esau married a woman outside the appropriate kinship boundaries. His wife was from the line of Ishmael, whose mother was not from within the patrilineage of Terah. This much is clear. From a genealogical point of view, what distinguishes Esau from Jacob is the character of their marriages. Rachel and Leah are correct wives for a son of the Abrahamic lineage because they are part of the collateral patrilineage of Nahor, as is Rebekah herself. But neither Mahalath nor any of Esau's other wives (Gen 26:34; 28:9) are part of this descent line; thus, Esau's marriage choices render him ineligible for inclusion in the Terahite patrilineage.

These stories illustrate the relationship between marriage and patrilineal descent. The emphasis on inheritance, both of lineage and of property, allows us to infer that marriages are formed to keep inheritance of land within certain kinship boundaries. The connection between marriage and inheritance is especially clear in Abraham's marriage to Keturah (Gen 25:1-6). After Sarah died, Abraham married another woman, Keturah, an additional wife who produced for Abraham six additional children, who themselves reproduced. Abraham recognizes his paternal responsibility to these children (and to children by other women; see v. 6) by providing them with "gifts." The text, however, emphasizes that "Abraham gave all that he had to Isaac" (v. 5), who lived totally apart from the offspring of Abraham's subsequent spouses. On the one hand, the statuses of Abraham's wives are separate from the statuses of their children—all of Abraham's children receive some material benefits from this biological relationship. On the other hand, only one son, Isaac, is confirmed as heir in the patrilineal descent of the Israelite lineage. Isaac functions as lineal heir not only because his mother had the correct genealogical relationship to his father, but also because Isaac chose (more correctly, was given) for a wife a woman with the correct kinship ties to his father's line—namely, Isaac and Rebekah are patrilineal collateral relations.

Examples from Genesis

The marriage pattern in Gen 11:10—50:26 is consistent with anthropological theory on kinship relationships:[13] social contexts that emphasize inheritance maintain endogamy. Marriage to an agnate, an individual related by patrilineal descent, results in isolation of the lineage in order to uphold a certain social status determined by property. In this type of marriage, a lineal heir can be created only by marriage with a daughter of collateral offspring. All of the women within the patrilineage of Abraham are ultimately members of the patrilineage of Terah, through his sons Abram, Nahor, and Haran. For example, the appropriateness of the marriage between Jacob and Rachel and between Jacob and Leah depends upon the fact that Laban, the women's father, is a son of Bethuel, who is a son of Nahor, who is a son of Terah. This pattern allows one to deduce that marriages based on patrilineal collateral descent from Terah through Abraham are endogamous; anthropological study of kinship groups supports the conclusion reached on the basis of the biblical data and maintains that endogamous marriage is regularly important when inheritance is the family's concern. By contrast, marriages of alliance are formed only between exogamous groups, which is palpably not the case in Gen 11:10—50:26.

One might concede the existence of a patrilineal descent system but object that there is also evidence of a matrilineal descent pattern.[14] Nonetheless, consideration of two problematic verses in

---

13. Two recent theoretical discussions of kinship relevant for this study are L. Holy, *Kinship, Honour and Solidarity* (Manchester: Manchester Univ. Press, 1989); C. C. Harris, *Kinship* (Minneapolis: Univ. of Minnesota Press, 1990). These books raise important theoretical questions about what the researcher "sees" when analyzing kinship. They distinguish between the meaning attributed to an action by a social actor and the meaning given to such action by the one undertaking the investigation. Neither actors nor authors are necessarily conscious of the social meaning that an anthropologist may discover in doing social analysis. Thus, the former may explain life in a different manner than the latter, who may be more aware of larger forces at work in the society. I am grateful to Timothy Bagley for bringing these two valuable works to my attention.

14. N. Jay, "Sacrifice, Descent and the Patriarchs," *VT* 38 (1988) 52–70; and idem, *Throughout Your Generations Forever: Sacrifice, Religion, and Paternity* (Chicago and London: Univ. of Chicago Press, 1992) 94–111. Jay is analyzing the stories from the perspective of the different sources' different historical contexts, whereas I am interested in how the final redactor has understood the dynamics of descent when bringing the putative narrative sources together. Jay's interest in

Genesis illustrates the primary analytic significance of patrilineal kinship organization. Although Gen 24:15, 24 clearly identify Rebekah as the daughter of Bethuel, who is son of Milcah, the wife of Abraham's brother Nahor (Rebekah is within the patrilineage), Gen 24:48 and 29:5 appear to report that Rebekah and Laban's father is actually Nahor.[15] Once we recognize that the emphasis in Genesis is on patrilineal descent from father to son and on patrilineal endogamy—that is, taking wives from within the patrilineal group—we can discern that in Gen 24:48 the narrator traces Rebekah's genealogy back to the apical ancestor, the ancestor from whom the descent line is traced, Nahor. In a similar way, when Jacob speaks about Laban (Gen 29:5), he makes clear that he is looking for a man from the patrilineage of Nahor. Nahor establishes the line of descent, rather than Rebekah the line of alliance. According to this interpretation of the narratives, women do not marry outside the patrilineage because correct marriages occur only within the patrilineage.

An examination of the marriage patterns from the perspective of patrilineal descent helps us to understand not only what occurs in the narratives but also what is left out. For example, the names of the wives of both Bethuel and Laban are omitted from the texts. If the purpose of marriage in the family stories of Genesis were to form alliances between groups through the women exchanged, these names would be crucially important.[16] But in these texts, marriage functions to establish descent—not alliance. Therefore, establishing descent through the correct father is primary, as can be seen when one discovers that Bethuel, the father of Rebekah and Laban, may be traced all the way back to his kin

the function of sacrifice leads her to the important distinction between biological reproduction and social reproduction. She argues that male descent through the biological mother is recognized but overcome by means of sacrifice. The result is the establishment of social reproduction traced through the man, who is now recognized as the child's father but who may or may not be the biological father. She notes that this social organization of the lineage is particularly important in contexts where there is inheritance of property.

15. Von Rad believes that Bethuel's name was a later addition intended to harmonize the narrative with the genealogy in Gen 25:20 (G. von Rad, *Genesis* [OTL; Philadelphia: Westminster, 1972] 257), while Westermann argues Gen 29:5 reflects a tradition different from the one in Genesis 24, where Bethuel is the father of Rebekah (C. Westermann, *Genesis 12–36* [Minneapolis: Augsburg, 1985] 463).

16. For further discussion of this issue, see chapter 4, below.

Nahor. That Rebekah returns to her mother's house in Gen 24:28 may suggest that her father has more than one wife.[17] Nonetheless, the basic point is: Rebekah descends from Bethuel. Rebekah, like all the "proper" wives named in the family stories, derives from the patrilineage of Terah, which extends through his three sons: Abram, Nahor, and Haran.

The marriage rule of patrilineal endogamy may also shed light on the enigmatic statement by Abraham that his wife Sarah is his sister (Gen 20:12).[18] Although Abraham's statement that Sarah is his half-sister through his father may be an example of fast-talking to get out of trouble, and no independent evidence establishes a consanguineal link (related by blood and descent) between Abraham and Sarah, one must consider the possibility that he could be telling the "truth," namely, expressing the reality of her place in a system of patrilineal endogamy[19]—that is, Sarah falls within the patrilineage of Terah and hence, even though she is Abraham's wife, she could also be called his sister. Sarah is both wife and kinswoman to Abraham.[20]

---

17. For an alternative perspective on this issue, see C. Meyers, "'To Her Mother's House': Considering a Counterpart to the Israelite Bêt 'āb," The Bible and the Politics of Exegesis (ed. D. Jobling et al.; Cleveland: Pilgrim Press, 1991) 42–44.

18. See Pitt-Rivers (J. A. Pitt-Rivers, "The Fate of Shechem or the Politics of Sex," The Fate of Shechem or the Politics of Sex [Cambridge Studies in Social Anthropology 19; Cambridge: Cambridge Univ. Press, 1977] 126–71) for a structural analysis of marriage in Genesis based on the "wife-sister problem." Pitt-Rivers argues that Abraham and Isaac used their wives as a means to form alliances because exogamy was a political mechanism necessary for "nomads" in the process of sedentarization. By contrast, in Genesis 34 the fate of Shechem in his marriage to Dinah depends upon the Israelite preference for endogamy once Jacob settled in the land.

19. Donaldson's study ("Kinship Theory") interprets barrenness in Genesis to signal a dysfunctional marriage relationship. Hence, Donaldson deduces that Sarah is barren because the relationship between Abraham and Sarah is incestuous (assuming that Sarah genuinely is Abraham's half-sister through their father [Gen 20:12]); their marriage, then, does not establish an alliance: it is a marriage between two people of the same patrilineage. A contrary example of "an incestuous relationship" characterized by fertility is, however, found in Genesis. If one follows Donaldson's understanding of Isaac as Rebekah's brother because her grandfather Nahor is the brother of Isaac's father, then the marriage relationship between Milcah and Nahor must be classified as incestuous. In this case a daughter is marrying her father, because Nahor is the brother of Milcah's father, Haran. But Milcah bears eight children (Gen 22:20-23), and as far as we know, with no biological obstacles such as infertility.

20. It appears then that both Abraham and Nahor take wives from within the patrilineage of their father, Terah.

The Structure of Marriage

Discussion of the relationship between marriage patterns and inheritance decisions in Genesis requires a brief survey of the various cross-cultural arrangements for sexual union in family and kinship groupings. Although monogamy is the type of marriage most familiar in our society, it may be a rather ineffective arrangement for perpetuation of the family due to the various potential obstacles that may interfere with reproduction.

There are several different options by means of which a family can cope with the absence of progeny. Serial monogamy occurs when a man divorces a barren woman in an attempt to marry a fertile one. Even more effective than serial monogamy for producing heirs is either polygyny or polycoity. Polygyny is defined as taking additional wives of equal status, as opposed to polycoity, which is the addition of concubines or handmaids—that is, women of lower status than the primary wife.[21] An option other than adding women is for a husband to add a child or children; in other words, he can adopt. The choice between these options is determined by issues such as custom, economics (property considerations), and the age of the parties to the primary marriage. The relationship between these options and the designation of the family heir in the Genesis narratives further depends upon both the man and the woman, whether a primary or a secondary wife, being descendants of the Terahite lineage. In the case of adoption in the biblical texts, the adopted individual must be able to trace his lineage back to Terah.

The socioeconomic distinctions between the sexual unions listed above affect the status differences between a primary wife and a concubine, a secondary wife. These distinctions are influenced by economic considerations; for example, a woman bringing property into the marriage (through either direct and/or indirect dowry) has legal and economic rights not available to a woman who does not bring in property. If a husband divorces a wife, the conjugal fund established at the time of their marriage

---

21. One notes that all of these labels categorize marriage from the male point of view. The expectation is for one husband to have one or more wives. In the situation of a woman married to more than one husband, the marriage is labeled as polyandry.

will be dissolved, and the husband will lose economic assets.[22] Hence, if a wife is barren, it may be more economically advantageous for the husband to remain married to the barren woman and to utilize a concubine for purposes of procreation. In this case, one must distinguish the status of the child borne by the concubine from the status of the concubine herself. Only in a situation where there are rival claims to heirship between the child of a primary wife and the child of a secondary wife do the child and its mother share the same status.

Our discussion of marriage transactions and status differentiation between wives and concubines should by now make it evident that these women have different roles. The basis for this distinction is chiefly economic. A primary wife is a woman whose continued status depends on whether there is a marital fund that was established when she was joined with her husband and that would be lost to him if the marriage were to be dissolved. The wife who is barren and who brings nothing into a marriage takes nothing out of it if she leaves.

A concubine, in this scheme, is a woman whose continued presence within the family is not dependent on economic arrangements. Typically a concubine is a secondary wife, a woman whose involvement with the husband represents a secondary union, both in terms of being an additional wife and of having a lower status than the legal wife. This secondary status means that a concubine herself has limited rights. In contemporary society, when a concubine and her child have limited rights, the union is referred to as "morganatic" marriage. Marriage between a husband and a concubine is made without difficulty and can be dissolved just as easily as it was formed.

A family unit can include both a wife and a concubine, or slave wife, and still be labeled a monogamous marriage. In fact, concubinage is typically associated with monogamy, not polygyny.[23] In the situation of a union between a man and a barren woman, a concubine may be used as a strategy for obtaining an heir because

---

22. The goods a woman brings to her marriage are both her "endowment" and her protection against divorce; see Goody, *Orient*, 345–46. For a general discussion of dowry in the Bible, see R. Westbrook, *Property and the Family in Biblical Law* (JSOTSup 113; Sheffield: JSOT Press, 1991) 142–64.

23. J. Goody, "Polygyny, Economy and the Role of Women," *The Character of Kinship* (ed. J. R. Goody; Cambridge: Cambridge Univ. Press, 1973) 180.

she does not threaten the economic basis for the marriage. She is brought into the family unit for maintaining generational continuity, not for building up the property of the family. Her secondary status as a slave wife is separated from the status of her child, who is considered a legitimate heir to its biological father, and to the primary wife, if she has contributed to the marital property.

The Function of Marriage: Economic Issues

Cross-cultural studies devoted to the social history of the family can be categorized into three major approaches: (1) those that focus on demographics; (2) those that concentrate on attitudes and sentiment; and (3) those based on household economics.[24] The studies based on household economics include analysis of inheritance by social anthropologists and examine family units and their patterns of individual behavior as a function of the survival of the family unit. The household, rather than its members, is the basic unit of analysis.[25] Individual actions are evaluated as representative of group interests insofar as an individual is a member of the family unit. Such an approach is concerned with both production and reproduction.

The family household is a social unit that maintains generational continuity while carrying out political, structural, and economic functions.[26] Decisions about property transmission and inheritance have a direct bearing on the shape of the family household and on family members' behavior.[27] The inheritance system

---

24. L. A. Tilly and M. Cohen, "Does the Family Have a History?" *Social Science History* 6 (1982) 131–79.

25. Lemche, *Early Israel*, 245–60; D. C. Hopkins, *The Highlands of Canaan* (Sheffield: Almond, 1985) 252. See C. Meyers (*Discovering Eve: Ancient Israelite Women in Context* [New York: Oxford Univ. Press, 1988] 128–64) for an in-depth discussion of the workings of the Israelite household.

26. For a study on the socioeconomic and religious life of Abraham as a seminomadic dweller (within a relatively confined area and definitely not as far as Mesopotamia), see U. Worschech, *Abraham: Eine sozialgeschichtliche Studie* (Europäische Hochschulschriften 23/225; Frankfurt: Peter Lang, 1983).

27. As Jay remarks, "Descent 'systems' are all ideal ways of ordering the social relations of reproduction, and, as is true of all forms of social organization, unilineal descent is associated with specific kinds of economic production. The varieties of enduring intergenerational continuity such groups strive for may be glossed as 'lineage' organization. Lineage organization is particularly efficient for

becomes a major factor in the timing of family fission. For example, in a context where all the family property passes to only one son (regardless of whether this is the firstborn son), disenfranchised male siblings will be forced to leave home at an early age to seek their own fortunes.[28] This situation obtains both in domestic units where the inheritance passes on after the father's death, and where it devolves upon an heir before the parent's death. The timing of the passing on of an inheritance may affect a man's ability to marry—for example, he may have the economic resources needed to contract a marriage only at the point of his father's death.[29]

The household economics approach raises questions that determine what behavior holds family members together and what behavior drives them apart. Household members' actions conform to societal rules on inheritance. Put another way, inheritance arrangements help explain family behavior. Inheritance arrangements will provide the interpretive framework for studying the variations in family structure described in Gen 11:10—50:26.

The household economics perspective is advantageous because it allows us to analyze human behavior not as representing individual temperament or choice but in terms of group ex-

---

control and transmission by inheritance of productive property such as farmland and livestock herds, and also of gainful monopolized skills, including priestly skills and political office" (*Throughout Your Generations*, 34). On the connection between inheritance and variation in household structure, see W. Goldschmidt and E. J. Kunkel, "The Structure of the Peasant Family," *American Anthropologist* 73 (1971) 1058–76. However, Goldschmidt and Kunkel argue that analysis of peasant family structure must also take into account ruling-class interests. On the subject of undivided inheritance in the Bible, see Westbrook, *Property and the Family*, 118–41.

28. L. E. Stager, "The Archaeology of the Family in Ancient Israel," *BASOR* 260 (1985) 25–28.

29. For a fascinating study on the connection between a man's age at marriage and the time of his father's death, see M. T. Roth, "Age at Marriage and the Household: A Study of Neo-Babylonian and Neo-Assyrian Forms," *Comparative Studies in Society and History* 29 (1987) 715–47. Roth demonstrates that while diverging life expectancies influence the age at which first marriage takes place, the relative difference between the spouses' ages will typically be somewhere over a decade. Although we obviously are unable to consider the inflated ages of individuals in Genesis as reliable indicators of life expectancy in ancient Israel, the age difference between Sarah and Abraham is in basic conformity with the data in Roth's study. Abraham is ten years older than Sarah, according to Gen 17:17.

pectations. In the present study, recurring behavior provides information on kinship interests that inform individual action. In speaking of patterned behavior I will not be limiting the discussion to the biblical material but will be attempting to locate household strategies on heirship within the wider context of ethnographic data. For example, Sarah's personality is of little interest here. Her conduct is important, however, because it communicates information regarding behavioral norms, roles for an Israelite woman—a primary wife—who is at first barren but who later bears an heir to her husband after a concubine has also provided him with a child.

I have just referred to group/kinship interests in the biblical texts; however, there is no denying that all women (and all men) do not share the same concerns—whether they lived in biblical Israel or live today—even if all women (and men) find themselves living in families at some point in their lives. In fact, a woman's interests may be in direct conflict with household needs. To argue otherwise would result in a reductionistic perspective. It would be more appropriate to note that individual and family interests intersect at various stages in the evolution of the family and the development of the individual.

In this study, the socioeconomic questions raised determine the focus of inquiry. For purposes of pursuing issues raised by the household economics approach, the unit of analysis is the household. However, this is not to diminish the importance of individual women's lives in ancient Israel—if, in fact, we can make judgments about them by relying on the Bible. I leave it to others to decide if the biblical record provides enough historical evidence to assess the lives of individual women and, if so, how that evidence is to be evaluated.[30] For the questions raised in this work, the appropriate level of analysis is the household as representative of collective interests.

---

30. The distinction between "biblical woman" and "Israelite woman" is discussed by Meyers, *Discovering Eve*, 4–6. Even if we are not presently able to locate actual marriage practices in ancient Israel, I assume that the Bible provides evidence of the ideology surrounding such behavior. Moreover, I assume a correspondence between the ideology in the texts and the society responsible for producing them while recognizing that the texts themselves are not historical documents.

The Family Structure

In order to understand better the economic functions of the household, it is important to discuss the structure of the family household and its place within Israelite society. As noted above, in speaking of family structure I am referring to the makeup of domestic life and examining the crucial unit, albeit the smallest or most basic level of social organization.[31] The household, the *bêt 'āb*, represents the daily life depicted in the Genesis narratives; yet the place of the household within a larger family grouping provides the context for emphasis on descent. It is important that one's discussion of family households in ancient Israel have the same analytic precision found in social-scientific studies on domestic groups. Terminology from the latter helps one bring the former into the larger context of studies on the history of the family.

A *family household* is a coresidential group comprised of a married couple, any of their unmarried children, and servants. The term may also apply to a widowed individual living with a child or children. The family household thus must include, at a minimum, either two spouses and an offspring or a widowed person and an offspring. An alternative label for this grouping is a nuclear family. Individuals less closely connected do not by themselves comprise a family household. Isaac, Rebekah, and their sons Jacob and Esau form a simple family household, or a nuclear family.

When more individuals, who are relatives, are added to the above grouping, it is referred to as an *extended family household*. An upwardly extended family household occurs when these additional kin are from a generation prior to the head of the household, for example, the father's mother. Conversely, a downwardly extended household refers to the presence of relatives from a generation younger than the head of the household. An extended family household, however, may contain only one conjugal pair. Here one thinks, for example, of the grouping formed of Abram, Sarah, and Lot.

---

31. Recent studies suggest that the tribe was not as important in Israelite social structure as had earlier been thought; see Lemche (*Early Israel*, 245–90) on social structure in premonarchical Israel. For a general discussion of the social world in the Hebrew Bible, consult D. L. Petersen, "The Social World of the Old Testament," *The Oxford Study Edition of the Revised English Bible* (ed. J. Suggs et al.; New York: Oxford Univ. Press, 1992) 68–78.

Lastly, the term *multiple-family household* refers to a domestic unit comprised of more than one conjugal pair. The couples must be linked either through marriage or descent.[32] Although the biblical evidence is ambiguous on this point, if Laban's wife was alive at the time when Jacob and his wives Rachel and Leah dwelt with Laban (who was their father), then the group would have comprised a multiple-family household. A clearer example, from outside of Genesis, occurs at the very beginning of the book of Ruth, when Naomi and Elimelek reside with their sons Mahlon and Chilion, and their wives Ruth and Orpah.

While the definitions used by social scientists in their discussions of residential units are precise, the same is not true when one studies the relevant and corresponding Hebrew terminology. Problems of interpretation result because the same Hebrew word appears to apply to more than one of the groupings delineated in the social sciences. I follow N. P. Lemche's work in understanding the *bêt 'āb* to be the smallest unit of society, one with a residential character, yet responsible for productive functions.[33] However, *bêt 'āb* apparently corresponds to more than one social unit, namely, both simple and extended family households,[34] and therefore requires further investigation when it occurs in the biblical text. For example, in the case of Jacob and sons (Gen 50:8), the meaning of *bêt 'ābîw* is ambiguous. The phrase may be interpreted to refer to either Jacob's nuclear family or his extended family. Moreover, according to Lemche, "*bêt 'āb* may be used of lineages and extended families, even though in sociological terms these are two distinct levels in societal structure. The extended family is a residential group, while the other, the lineage, is a descent group which is composed of a number of residential groups."[35] Thus, in Gen 28:21, when Jacob speaks of returning to *bêt 'ābî*, it is unclear whether he means his father's extended family or his father's lin-

---

32. P. Laslett, "Introduction: The History of the Family," *Household and Family in Past Time* (ed. P. Laslett and R. Wall; Cambridge: Cambridge Univ. Press, 1972) 28–32.

33. On this point, see also N. K. Gottwald, *The Tribes of Yahweh: A Sociology of the Religion of Liberated Israel, 1250–1050 B.C.E.* (Maryknoll, N.Y.: Orbis Books, 1979) 292.

34. Lemche's analysis lacks precision on this point for its failure to distinguish between extended and multiple-family households. He collapses the two household forms into the category of "extended family."

35. Lemche, *Early Israel,* 252.

eage group. Further, more than one lineage may occupy the same town.

Therefore, one can speak of the *bêt 'āb* as the primary unit of analysis in the ancestral stories, recognizing that heirship to the *bêt 'āb* confers both residential and lineage rights. When Isaac becomes Abraham's lineal heir, the descent line of Terah passes through him, and he receives his father's property. By contrast, the other children of Abraham, Ishmael and the offspring of Keturah (Gen 25:1-6), must live far away from Isaac and are not lineal heirs of Terah. They are no longer members of Abraham's *bêt 'āb*.

Based upon close scrutiny of the biblical terms, Lemche concludes that the *mišpāḥâ*, "the maximal lineage (or possibly, the clan),"[36] is less significant for understanding social structure in ancient Israel. The *mišpāḥâ* is the enlargement of the kinship circle to include lineages related by marriage. On a daily basis, an individual in ancient Israel would be less directly affected by the *mišpāḥâ* and more acutely aware of his or her position within the *bêt 'āb*. In fact, Lemche questions the political nature of the term *mišpāḥâ* and does not believe it has a residential base.[37]

Thus, the family household, the *bêt 'āb*, refers to both social organization and residency. A family household is a domestic unit, a group of persons living together who are related by birth or marriage (though servants may also be included in the unit) and who depend upon each other for purposes of economic survival. As noted, although biblical scholars have attempted to understand better the organization of the Israelite household, the texts themselves provide conflicting evidence on this issue; even the archaeological data can be ambiguous. Modern interpreters may have information on how ancient homes were laid out and on how public buildings or utilities were placed, and yet it is still difficult to be certain of how the people who inhabited these spaces utilized them. Moreover, social scientists inform us that in any society no one form of social organization predominates. The texts that concern us, the ancestral stories, present information on a variety of

---

36. Ibid., 269.
37. See Gottwald, *Tribes*, 257-70, on the protective function of the *mišpāḥâ* in premonarchic times.

household forms. Yet due to family fission, residential forms are never static but give rise to new configurations in the course of the evolution of the family household.

Despite the diversity of family households depicted in Genesis, the stories about these units share a common socioeconomic concern. Family households devise and maintain strategies for the economic and social survival of both the individual and *bêt 'āb*. On the basis of cross-cultural studies of the history of the family, we can discover that a means for ensuring survival includes the retention and extension of property; here one thinks of Abraham's argument with Abimelech over water rights (Gen 21:25-34). Property, especially land, needs to be retained within the family household; it is to be transferred intact from one generation to the next. Fragmentation of family holdings diminishes the family's ability to survive economically and socially. From the perspective of the household economics approach, strategies to achieve this survival are the subject of the narratives in Gen 11:10—50:26. These strategies are central to the function of the Israelite family household.

I understand the emphasis on property and socioeconomic survival in the ancestral texts to conform to models of peasant society and social organization. The term *peasants* is used here to refer to farmers working the land. For purposes of this study, peasants are defined as individuals who have rights to the land that they farm—that is, they are farmers who work their own land and whose sustenance is dependent on this work. They are not oriented toward a market economy. In a peasant culture, economic survival and social status are attached to property and property rights.

One may speak of a peasant society without regard for the political basis of the society. A peasant can be either a free farmer— that is, one who controls the products of his labor—or a farmer subject to a political hierarchy that exploits his work. In the following chapters, political concerns will be bracketed until the conclusions are formulated, because, regardless of the political context, one of the functions of the family household is to provide an heir to inherit this property. Domestic units provide the context for ensuring this social and economic development, as well as family continuity from one generation to the next.

Land and Property

Explicit in the household economics approach is a concern with property in general and land in particular. Moreover, the approach focuses on the relationship between descent and inheritance decisions. I have already demonstrated that descent is a central concern in Genesis. Based on comparative ethnographic studies, one would assume that this emphasis on proper lineage ties in Genesis is maintained in order to guarantee that inheritance passes into the appropriate hands. But does inheritance in the case of the Hebrew Bible refer to more than just the inheritance of the name of the lineage? Is land actually a concern in these texts? In their canonical position, the ancestral texts speak of the promise of land; but this is a promise that reaches fulfillment several books later, many generations after Abraham.

Despite the initial impression of a situation of landlessness created by the emphasis on promise in Genesis, a closer reading of the texts reveals that property and even conflict caused by excessive wealth are major concerns in the narratives. The stories abound with references to material goods, to the friction between individuals that results over them, and to family household fission as a result of this abundance. Sometimes this conflict is intergenerational; other times it is not. Abraham's extended family household increases as a result of his sojourn in Egypt (Gen 12:10—13:1); and we learn that immediately after this episode "Lot, who went with Abram, also had flocks and herds and tents, so that the land could not support both of them dwelling together; for their possessions were so great that they could not live together" (Gen 13:6-7). Due to increasing wealth, fission of the multiple-family household is also the fate of Esau and his brother Jacob in Gen 36:6-7: "Then Esau took his wives, his sons, his daughters, and all the members of his household, his cattle, all his beasts, and all his property which he had acquired in the land of Canaan; and he went into a land away from his brother Jacob. For their possessions were too great for them to dwell together; the land of their sojournings could not support them because of their cattle." Ultimately, Jacob leaves his uncle, Laban, over property conflicts that also involve the rights of Laban's sons and daughters to family property (Genesis 31). Family households are fractured due to tensions over property rights.

Similarly, the matter of property claims extends beyond family household boundaries to larger residential groups. In Gen 21:25-34, Abraham and Abimelech quarrel over competing water rights to a well. By contrast, in Gen 34:10, Jacob and Hamor make a treaty to live together with the mutual sharing of property—though both parties already appear to be wealthy. Hence, we may observe that despite the apparent emphasis on the future realization of the promise of land, the ancestors are far from impoverished. Questions of property and wealth appear central throughout the family stories. And where there is family property, inheritance rights, established by kinship ties, are important.

In short, on the one hand, the texts present a picture of the future realization of the promise of land, but, on the other hand, they portray individuals in possession of significant wealth (material goods and domestic servants—movable property) and land (immovable property such as the well in Gen 21:25-34). The one notable exception in the matter of property concerns Abraham's need to purchase a piece of land in order to bury his dead wife Sarah (Genesis 23). Interestingly, he possesses the number of shekels (400)[38] required to complete the transaction with the Hittites. Land is important, then, but not the only material good relevant to inheritance claims in Genesis.

It is intriguing that, despite the surface appearances, matters relating to landholdings and property pervade the texts of Gen 11:10—50:26. Cross-cultural data suggest that rights of land inheritance appear to explain why Isaac cannot go back to the "old country" but must remain in Canaan at all costs at the time he takes a bride; if the kinswoman is unwilling to return with the servant, Isaac cannot go to her (Genesis 24). Inheritance is patrilocal; it depends upon the heir residing in his father's family house-

---

38. Abraham diplomatically negotiates to buy a burial spot for Sarah and ends up not only with the cave of Machpelah, but with the entire field in which it lies. Although Ephron first insists that Abraham should take the land for free (vv. 10-11), Abraham ultimately pays for this putative gift. In contrast to the 400 shekels Abraham spends, Jeremiah buys land for 17 shekels (Jer 32:9), while Omri purchases the land for building Samaria at the rate of 2 talents of silver, or 6000 shekels (1 Kgs 16:24). On the price of the cave of Machpelah, Westbrook (*Property and the Family*, 24 n. 1) comments, "On the generally accepted assumption that 400 shekels was an exorbitant price we may only comment that any conclusion about the price is altogether impossible. Without knowledge of the contemporary value of money or the size of the land we lack the barest criteria for assessment."

hold.[39] The situation is that Isaac must remain on the land of his father, Abraham. The situation of multiple offspring (Ishmael and Isaac, and Jacob and Esau) inevitably leads to the separation of brothers to different lands. This is because of a concern that the family land not be divided; land as livelihood requires that the property remain intact—that is, as large as possible—to insure economic survival.

Inheritance

Biblical legislation on inheritance aims to preserve family land; the terms of the laws are based on patrilocal residence patterns. The preferred list of heirs to the father's land is as follows: son, daughter, brother, father's brother. If none of the preceding is alive, the next surviving kinsman is recognized as heir (Num 27:8-11). In the interest of preserving family land intact—that is, not dividing it into smaller and smaller tracts—Deut 21:17 maintains the rights of the primogeniture, according to which the firstborn is to inherit twice as much as his brothers. This law should be upheld even if the firstborn son is borne by a less favored wife in the father's household (Deut 21:15-17). However, the nonlegal biblical texts of Genesis present a picture of inheritance practices at odds with those in the legal material.[40]

The transmission of property from one generation to the next is an important concern in Genesis. For example, this interest in inheritance is reported at the end of Abraham's life when we learn that upon his death, "Abraham gave all he had to Isaac. But to the sons of his concubines Abraham gave gifts, and while he was still alive he sent them away from his son Isaac, eastward to the east country" (Gen 25:5-6). The separation between Isaac and the other offspring of Abraham guarantees that the former's

---

39. This residence requirement explains the provision allowing the daughters of Zelophehad to inherit from their father, so long as they marry a local kinsman (Num 36:6).

40. For an attempt to reconcile narrative and law, see C. Carmichael, *Women, Law, and the Genesis Traditions* (Edinburgh: Edinburgh Univ. Press, 1979); idem, *Law and Narrative in the Bible: The Evidence of the Deuteronomic Laws and the Decalogue* (Ithaca, N.Y.: Cornell Univ. Press, 1985). In his analysis of biblical law on property and family, Westbrook (*Property and the Family*) provides a thorough discussion of the legal material, but his work needs to be nuanced based on cross-cultural, social-scientific study of these issues.

inheritance will not be threatened by challenges from the latter. Moreover, in the Genesis narratives property is not only transmitted to sons; daughters also are the recipients of goods from their families. This fact appears to explain the complaint by Rachel and Leah when Jacob tries to persuade them to return with him to his homeland. In Gen 31:14-16, the two daughters of Laban agree to Jacob's request because their father has unjustly deprived them of their inheritance property (v. 14, ḥēleq wĕnaḥălâ).

Cross-cultural data reveal that diverging devolution, transmission of property through both sons and daughters, is associated with endogamy—the form of marriage attested in Genesis. Endogamous marriage practices keep property isolated within the kinship group. A policy of endowing both sons and daughters, beyond guaranteeing household socioeconomic stability, is linked to concerns with the economic status of the household. The status of a daughter is maintained through the property she receives as a dowry from her parents but is enhanced by gifts from the groom's family. One need only think of the lavish gifts Abraham's servant bestows upon Rebekah, as well as on her family, when he arranges her marriage to Isaac (Genesis 24). The passage of material goods from the family of the groom to the family of the bride should not lead one to think of women as "property" exchanged between men. When these gifts are analyzed from a cross-cultural perspective, one can see that they serve as a means of maintaining status differentiation—that is, they link a man and a woman from comparable economic backgrounds.[41] Moreover, honor accrues to the bride's family when they find a groom for her who will keep her in the style to which she has become accustomed.

In contexts where women typically do not inherit land, the dowry a woman receives from her family can serve as her inheritance; she receives this inheritance at the time of her marriage, rather than upon the death of her father. As Goody puts it: this practice "is likely to appear in societies in which status is based on economic differentiation. Indeed it is both a cause and effect of a certain type of stratification. When differences of economic status emerge, when one wants to control the marriages of daughters or sisters in terms of that status, then dowry is the characteristic

---

41. Goody, *Production and Reproduction*, 11–15.

of marriage transactions."[42] Thus, in an endogamous marriage, the marriage arrangement is not only designed to keep property within the family but is also linked with status. Endogamy is a marriage strategy that results in social isolation in order to guarantee that an individual finds a spouse from the desired socioeconomic and lineage background. By contrast, when daughters do not inherit in any way, there is little reason for parents to exercise control over their marriage choices. I will return to this point later and consider whether or not this economic fact explains the course of events in the story of the rape of Dinah (Genesis 34). The link between kinship and property appears to have a bearing not only on how and where Israelite men are expected to find appropriate women for marriage partners, but on who proper men for Israelite women to marry might be.

At this point in the discussion it is necessary to distinguish between direct and indirect dowry. The former refers to material goods passed from parents to their daughter upon her marriage. The latter refers to what the groom gives the bride as gifts. Gifts from the groom's family to the bride's family, commonly known as brideprice or bridewealth, can be given to the bride by her father or be passed on when the bride's brother desires to contract a marriage. In no way do these gifts signify that the bride is understood as chattel sold from one family to the next.[43]

When the bride moves from her home to the household of the groom, as happens in Genesis with Rebekah and eventually with Rachel and Leah, women do not inherit land. The one exception in the Hebrew Bible, the case of the daughters of Zelopehad (Num 27:1-11; 36:5-12), allows women to inherit land provided they marry someone locally.[44] If we consider the issue from a cross-cultural perspective, we discover that women who inherit land are able to reverse marriage residence patterns (women moving to the groom's household) and attract men to their family households.[45]

---

42. Ibid., 23.

43. Ibid., 10–11. Goody restudies these issues (*Orient*) and argues that ethnocentric Western biases assume an evolutionary development from the "primitive" East to the "civilized" West and cloud our judgment on the nature of marriage in contexts removed from our own. In the case of the biblical material, marriage should be analyzed within the framework of the inheritance system argued for in the present study.

44. Lemche, *Early Israel*, 259.

45. Goody, *Production and Reproduction*, 18.

Whether the bride brings movable or immovable property, in contexts such as Genesis where marriage is an economic arrangement, the property of a man and a woman are joined in a marital fund at the time of their union. A groom's gifts to his bride are included in this fund, as well as the direct dowry she brings from her family. This fund becomes the basis for the bond between them.

Often implicit in the emphasis on keeping property within a circumscribed boundary of kinship is the fact of limited resources. If unlimited plots of land existed there would be no rationale for passing immovable property intact from one generation to the next. Individuals might otherwise "homestead" on unclaimed land. The same is true of movable property. It appears that limitations on available resources provide one explanation for highly developed systems of inheritance designed to perpetuate social and economic organization. Here, one again thinks of the fact that Isaac lives far away from the other potential claimants to Abraham's inheritance. Or, to take another example, in Genesis 31, Laban's sons appear to fear that their inheritance from their father will be jeopardized by Jacob's claims to this property, due to his success with livestock.

Inheritance decisions condition interpersonal relationships within the family as well as the configuration of the household. Factors to consider in these household dynamics include the stage in the development of the family when the inheritance is passed on from one generation to the next, and the size of the inheritance. Two assumptions are implicit in this statement: (1) the family is a social unit that changes over time; and (2) in the absence of family property there is no rationale for maintaining kinship ties or for emphasizing descent. Cross-cultural data indicate that kinship ties are reinforced in the presence of family property.[46] Exogamy, marriage outside the kinship group, is an attractive option for those lacking property; it is an important means for increasing one's

---

46. "It is clear to anyone who has worked with family reconstitution in villages where there is a peasant landholding class that godparents are chosen on anything but a casual basis. Where there is no property there is no basis for emphasizing ties of kinship that already exist, that is in reinforcing ties of blood or affinity as social ties, nor for creating new ties that are expected to be of long duration" (D. Sabean, "Aspects of Kinship and Behaviour and Property in Rural Western Europe before 1800," *Family and Inheritance* [ed. J. Goody et al.; Cambridge: Cambridge Univ. Press, 1976] 98).

holdings. At least that is the argument Hamor, father of Shechem, uses in Gen 34:9-10 when he attempts to convince Jacob to allow his daughter Dinah to marry Shechem.

A family member could inherit both movable and immovable goods. In a peasant (that is, an agrarian-based) community, land, immovable wealth, is the most valuable resource one can inherit because it provides the means for economic survival. Therefore, the strategy for ensuring the survival of the household is to avoid breaking up the land at the time when it passes from one generation to the next. As noted earlier, in contexts when only one sibling inherits land (again, see Gen 25:6), other offspring must find other economic options for making a livelihood. Moreover, analysis of family history must also consider the stage in the household's development when the lineal heir takes possession of the inheritance. If household survival depends on ownership of land (for example, in an agricultural society where it is the means of production and consequently of reproduction), an heir might be able to marry only at the time of acquisition of land. Age at marriage will then be linked to transference of property. Issues such as these may give rise to generational conflict. Here one thinks of Isaac's advanced age when he decides to confer "blessing" on firstborn Esau and the tension that results between Jacob and Esau over matters relating to lineal heirship (Genesis 27).

Anthropological Models and Historical Reconstruction

Thus far we have been concerned with cross-cultural data and the potential relevance they have for illumining Gen 11:10—50:26. But where do anthropology and history meet in the study of the ancestral texts? Specifically, do cross-cultural models help us study, and attempt to date, texts that purport to speak about ancient Israelite origins? The texts may have historical roots, yet they might as likely be ideological projections from a later time. There is the problem of the chronological gap separating the events described in Genesis and the final shaping of the texts. The final use of the text may represent ideological or theological concerns of this later setting, rather than concerns of the patriarchs' and matriarchs' original situation. How much importance should scholars attach to the historical gap between the events described in the texts and the final date of the texts and the circumstances in which they were shaped? Do these models help in resolving issues of historical reconstruction?[47]

Probably no issue regarding the texts in Genesis has captured the mind of the historical-biblical critic as much as that of the historicity of the patriarchs and matriarchs. Some scholars assert that the texts concerning the ancestral period reflect life in the second millennium (Middle Bronze Age),[48] while others argue that they address concerns of the exilic period in Israel's history.[49] Others have gone so far as to maintain that there never was a time in Israel's past that historically corresponds to the so-called patriarchal period.[50] In this ongoing debate, some scholars base their arguments on archaeological data; others appeal to literary considerations. The scholarly waters of historical criticism are presently muddy on the issues relating to the historicity and dating of the background presumed in Gen 11:10—50:26. It is not unreasonable to assert that theories concerning the putative historicity of the ancestral narratives are as numerous as the scholars who propose them.

A work of Thomas L. Thompson was one of the pioneering studies in recent historical-critical scholarship concerned with the question of whether or not Genesis is a reliable source for historical reconstruction of Israel's prehistory.[51] I discuss it not so

---

47. Presently in biblical scholarship there is much interest in understanding the biblical reconstruction of ancient Israelite history. Seminal works include J. van Seters, *In Search of History: Historiography in the Ancient World and the Origins of Biblical History* (New Haven: Yale Univ. Press, 1983); idem, *Prologue to History: The Yahwist as Historian in Genesis* (Louisville: Westminster/John Knox Press, 1992); the essays collected in P. R. Davies and D. M. Gunn, eds., "The History of Ancient Israel and Judah: A Discussion of Miller-Hayes (1986)," *JSOT* 39 (1987) 3–63; G. Garbini, *History and Ideology in Ancient Israel* (New York: Crossroad, 1988); B. Halpern, *The First Historians* (San Francisco: Harper & Row, 1988); N. P. Lemche, *Ancient Israel: A New History of Israelite Society* (The Biblical Seminar 5; Sheffield: JSOT, 1988); R. Coote and D. Ord, *The Bible's First History* (Philadelphia: Fortress, 1989).

48. Most recently this dating is defended by Worschech, *Abraham*. Worschech is most useful for understanding social models, rather than for dating Genesis. His scholarship relies upon the traditional analysis of the pentateuchal sources J (the Yahwist), E (the Elohist), D (the Deuteronomist), and P (the Priestly Writer).

49. See, for example, J. van Seters, *Abraham in History and Tradition* (New Haven: Yale Univ. Press, 1975) 263–78.

50. So M. Clark: "The patriarchal period is a theological construct" ("The Patriarchal Traditions," *Israelite and Judaean History* [ed. J. H. Hayes and J. M. Miller; Philadelphia: Westminster, 1977] 147).

51. T. L. Thompson, *The Historicity of the Patriarchal Narratives: The Quest for the*

much for the historical conclusions it reaches, but for the historical questions it raises. Thompson's study was one of the first
to seriously challenge traditional scholarly understanding of the
ancestral stories and the dating of the narrative sources that comprise these texts. After having mounted an exhaustive review and
critique of archaeological, historical, linguistic, and legal material from the ancient Near East and Palestine in the first part of
the second millennium, Thompson then offers an in-depth analysis of eight alleged parallels between legal and social customs at
Nuzi and ancient Israel. His highly detailed study leads Thompson to the same negative conclusions reached by J. Wellhausen
at the end of the last century.[52] Based on the evidence available, Genesis cannot be historically verified. The impossibility of
reconstructing the historical background presupposed in the ancestral stories of Genesis results, avers Thompson, from the fact
that these texts are retrojections of the Yahwist in the monar-
chical period and are intended to give the Israelite nation an
ancestry.[53] In reaching these conclusions, Thompson challenges
not only the specific arguments traditionally used to relate the
ancestors to the Middle Bronze Age, but also the theoretical
principles involved in this historical reconstruction. According
to Thompson, the blame lies with scholars who have harmo-
nized ancient Near Eastern material from the second millennium
with the texts in Genesis as the result of a false analogy. He argues that scholars too quickly accepted the second millennium
as the historical and cultural background against which the patriarchs and matriarchs should be viewed. Once this period was
accepted by scholars, they then attempted to harmonize the external evidence provided by archaeology with the internal witness
of the biblical narratives. This questionable analogy prevented
past historical-critical studies from concluding, as Thompson
and others now do, that the historicity of the patriarchal nar-

---

Historical Abraham (BZAW 133; Berlin: de Gruyter, 1974). One might also consider
the works of van Seters (*Abraham in History*) and D. B. Redford (*A Study of the
Biblical Story of Joseph [Genesis 37–50]* [VTSup 20; Leiden: E. J. Brill, 1970]) in this
same context.

52. J. Wellhausen, *Prolegomena to the History of Ancient Israel* (New York:
Meridian Books, 1957). German original, 1878.

53. Thompson, *Historicity*, 324. Of course, the dating of the Yahwist, if such a
source exists, is presently in question.

ratives is not verifiable based on the evidence in the Hebrew Bible.[54]

Because there are as yet no good grounds for making definitive statements concerning the historicity and dating of the ancestral narratives, it is important to separate issues of dating and historical background from the fact that the stories under consideration reflect their authors' attempts to describe what they understood about Israelite experience in legitimate social contexts. Questions of historical validity, such as Thompson raises, can obscure what those responsible for shaping these texts brought into view through these traditions. Thompson himself recognizes that the traditions were not intended to be read historically. "They are rather sociological, political and religious."[55] For the time being, then, I will be bracketing questions of chronology in order to address the relevance of the application of social-scientific models to the history of the family.

Although I have established the difficulty of using higher critical studies to reconstruct Israelite history on the basis of biblical narratives, I should add that comparative data reveal that origin traditions such as one finds in Genesis are often the most recently added texts intended to justify later conditions.[56] They are often retrojections of later conditions into an earlier period. With this in mind, I will give priority to Genesis as conveying important information concerning inheritance of land as an issue within the framework of the texts. The situation may be that the narratives preserve ancient traditions; yet the final shaping of the biblical material is the context for understanding this material. To the extent that my utilization of the household economics model allows me to reach historical conclusions, the latter may not reflect the earliest history of the biblical traditions but may concern the sociological issues connected to the final shaping of these narratives. Thus, the texts may be important sources for historical reconstruction. They will not necessarily tell us what did or did not happen;

---

54. Thompson, *Historicity*, 1–21, 315–26; J. M. Miller and J. H. Hayes, *A History of Ancient Israel and Judah* (Philadelphia: Westminster, 1986) 75.

55. Thompson, *Historicity*, 315.

56. K. W. Whitelam, "Israel's Traditions of Origin: Reclaiming the Land," *JSOT* 44 (1989) 19–42; J. Vansina, "Comment: Traditions of Genesis," *Journal of African History* 15 (1974) 317–22; E. Hobsbawm and T. Ranger, *The Invention of Tradition* (Cambridge: Cambridge Univ. Press, 1983).

rather they convey information about self-understanding—that is, ancient Israelite ideology on ancestry.[57] I will postpone discussion of the dating of these texts until the final chapter, after literary-critical judgments are brought into my analysis of Gen 11:10—50:26.

In summary, much of my theoretical concern regarding analysis and use of these texts is encapsulated in a statement by Prewitt:

> For even with the precision of kinship relationships posited in the text, it is unlikely that we can differentiate actual historical process from practical political assertions which are mainly fictional. . . . If by "historical conclusions" we refer to a process of establishing historicity of Genesis narratives, I doubt we shall ever engage in such a process. On the other hand, if "historical conclusions" refer to assessment of the communities responsible for the narrative composition, I am more optimistic.[58]

---

57. Van Seters, *In Search of History*, 361. On the fact that the ancestral texts can be labeled as mythology or legend by biblical scholars and yet convey information on kinship, Oden writes, "Kinship and lineage provide the central focus or structure in many myths because both myths and kinship systems can be viewed as systems of communication" (*Bible without Theology*, 114).

58. Prewitt, *Elusive Covenant*, 31. This point is emphasized throughout Prewitt's work. He makes these comments in discussion of Oden's *Bible without Theology*. Although Prewitt's argument presupposes that marriage is for purposes of alliance, rather than for establishing descent, I agree with his understanding of the Genesis texts as social models.

Chapter 2

The Sarah-Hagar Cycle: Polycoity

Methodological Concerns

The following exposition of family life will follow the canonical order of the stories in Genesis, especially since the arrangement of the pericopes in their final form corresponds to the course of events in a family's history. The organization of the narratives is consistent with the normal developmental cycle of a family. When comparing the biblical material with cross-cultural data on family life in preindustrial, non-Western societies, there appear to be similarities at particular stages in the family's evolution. As we shall see, the biblical stories are concerned with only certain stages in the family cycle. Patterns that have been observed at specific points in the normal family history in other contexts are not consistently found in the biblical material. For example, other than notification that such stages occur in people's lives, there is little information in Genesis on pregnancy and birth, child rearing, and adolescence. These matters do not serve the interests of the biblical editors.

The following analysis is based on the thesis that the plot of Gen 11:10—50:26 unfolds through narratives that are set within a genealogical framework. The narratives and the genealogical framework together organize the plot of generational continuity.

Regarding the use of literary-critical insights to support this thesis, I will proceed on the assumption that the reality portrayed in the biblical story can be discerned only when the text is seen as composed of interrelated episodes that advance and supplement the plot. Literary-critical readings of the text will be interpreted in light of data from comparative kinship studies. The complementary use of kinship studies and literary-critical analysis yields new insights on the social structure of ancient Israel. For example, from a literary perspective, Sarah's barrenness in Genesis 12–21 serves as a means of maintaining narrative suspense. Will the promise given to Abraham by Yahweh in chapter 12 ever be realized given Sarah's infertility? When we move to comparative material from anthropology and sociology, we discover that the occurrence of Sarah's barrenness requires a context for exploring alternate options available to Abraham for designating an heir. The two perspectives complement each other in elucidating the function of barrenness in the stories about the marriage of Abraham and Sarah.[1] Or, to take another example, what, from literary analysis, is identified as the theme of promise of progeny can be understood from a cross-disciplinary perspective as a study of kinship and reproduction. Ultimately, the two approaches support each other in emphasizing a concern with family continuity.

Such interest in kinship and family is found in both narrative and genealogy. While genealogy functions in a social setting as lineage linkages, some of which may be artificial within their present literary setting in Genesis, genealogy also represents the unproblematic, uninterrupted continuity of family life. In Genesis 11–50, genealogy and narratives together focus on family concerns; the unifying issue of "family" allows us to identify these stories as belonging to the genre of "ancestral" or "family stories." Further, narratives then take on meaning by being read in the context of genealogy. For example, the repercussions of the possibility

---

1. For a discussion of the methodological difficulties inherent in the use of comparative data to analyze biblical material, see R. R. Wilson, *Prophecy and Society in Ancient Israel* (Philadelphia: Fortress, 1980) 15–16.

that Abraham may sacrifice his son Isaac in Genesis 22 become meaningful only if one is aware of Sarah's barrenness (Gen 11:30) and of the long wait that preceded Isaac's birth. Were Isaac to die, given Sarah's condition, it is highly unlikely that she would bear another son. Further, there is the contextual information that Abraham's other son, Ishmael, has already been expelled from the household. Without this knowledge the genealogical concerns adumbrated in Genesis 22 would be lost. The text might touch emotions about the loss of a child, but, removed from its family setting, the poignancy of Abraham's willingness to sacrifice his heir would lose significance.

Just as my analysis depends on the complementarity of scholarly approaches, it also seeks meaning within the literary world of the text through the integration of genealogy and narrative as they appear in Genesis. As noted above, both genealogy and narrative record family relations. They both relay information about family. Yet they convey meaning in different ways. Genealogy has no depth of meaning, is orderly, and presents generational continuity without interruption. By contrast, narrative has depth of meaning, is not orderly, and, in Genesis, deals with questions and problems challenging generational continuity.[2] But while this distinction between narrative and genealogy is necessary, within the context of Genesis, the two have a symbiotic relationship with the result that our interpretation of the texts comes from their juxtaposition and structural organization.[3]

As I will demonstrate further below, the genealogical material in the family stories of Genesis has been organized around three

---

2. R. B. Robinson, "Literary Functions of the Genealogies of Genesis," *CBQ* 48 (1986) 601–2; J. Scharbert, "Der Sinn der Toledot-Formel in der Priesterschrift," *Wort-Gebot-Glaube: Beiträge zur Theologie des Alten Testaments* (ed. H. J. Stoebe et al.; ATANT 59; Zurich: Zwingli, 1970) 52.

3. This same argument—that is, that a holistic reading of Genesis through the relationship between genealogy and narrative will provide us with an understanding of kinship issues—appears in T. J. Prewitt, *The Elusive Covenant* (Bloomington and Indianapolis: Indiana Univ. Press, 1990). Prewitt is interested in applying structural anthropology to analyze the political implications of kinship on the national level. Although we are interested in different levels of social analysis, and apply different anthropological approaches, there is much overlap between Prewitt's conclusions and my own. For an alternative view of narrative structure in Genesis, based on a functional theory of narrative, see H. C. White, *Narration and Discourse in the Book of Genesis* (Cambridge: Cambridge Univ. Press, 1991) 93–112.

narrative cycles, groups of stories about particular ancestors—for example, Abraham and Sarah—that exhibit the same basic skeletal order. The stories comprising these three cycles move genealogical concerns forward until the point where one cycle of literature ends and a new genealogy begins.[4] For example, the genealogy in 25:12-26, which introduces the stories of Isaac and his family, occurs only after death of his parents Sarah (Genesis 23) and Abraham (25:7-11). The narratives about Isaac's adult life are introduced when there is some complication in the genealogy—for example, when Rebekah's barrenness in 25:21 raises questions of whether a lineal heir will be found for Isaac; from the perspective of family history, a problem or question arises such that the direction of the genealogy is uncertain. To follow up on the preceding example, when Rebekah's barrenness is reversed and she gives birth to twin sons, it is still necessary to determine which of these two boys will be designated as his father's lineal heir. The narratives unfold until the point where the continuance of the genealogy has been resolved. Only then does narrative give way to another block of genealogical material. Narrative is another means of determining genealogical direction—that is, establishing heirship. Working out the literary concern with heirship provides the framework for extracting principles of kinship.

---

4. Several recent studies attempt to find structural cohesiveness in Genesis. For differing analyses of the structural pattern in the life histories of Abraham, Isaac, and Jacob, see E. Fox, "Can Genesis Be Read as a Book?" *Semeia* 46 (1989) 31–40; and L. R. Fisher, "The Patriarchal Cycles," *Orient and Occident: Essays Presented to Cyrus H. Gordon on the Occasion of His Sixty-Fifth Birthday* (ed. H. A. Hoffner; AOAT 22; Neukirchen-Vluyn: Neukirchener Verlag, 1973) 59–65. Neither of these authors accounts for the structural pattern in 12–50 in terms of the genealogies that the narratives are organized around. L. H. Silberman ("Listening to the Text," *JBL* 102 [1983] 3–26) speaks of narrative cycles and argues that the plot of Genesis is that of the "True Heir" without ever commenting on the relationship of the genealogical material to this concern. The boundaries he uses for the narrative cycles in the family stories do not agree with the divisions delineated in the present study. An excellent resource for those interested in the exegetical conclusions that arise when Genesis is understood as a literary unity is found in G. W. Coats, *Genesis with an Introduction to Narrative Literature* (Forms of the Old Testament Literature 1; Grand Rapids, Mich.: Eerdmans, 1983). See also, T. L. Thompson, *The Origin Tradition of Ancient Israel, I: The Literary Formation of Genesis and Exodus 1–23* (JSOTSup 55; Sheffield: Sheffield Academic, 1987). On persons' ages as the key to unlocking the structural organization in the "Abraham Cycle," see J. P. Fokkelman, "Time and the Structure of the Abraham Cycle," *OTS* 25 (1989) 96–109.

Genealogy and Resolving Heirship

Genesis 11:10-26

The division between primeval and ancestral history traditionally has been located at Gen 11:27, where the genealogy of Terah
begins.[5] Here, so Westermann argues, the story narrows down
to one family whose genealogy establishes the transition from
universal to Israelite history. My argument—that is, that there
is another possibility for interpreting the literary organization of
the family stories—depends upon including Gen 11:10-26 within
the boundaries of these stories. The result of beginning the ancestral history with this genealogy is the following outline: three
pairs of genealogical segments framing three narrative blocks.
This formulation allows us to see Gen 11:10-32 as the introduction to the stories in 12:1—25:11; Gen 25:12-26 as the introduction
to the stories in 25:27—35:29; and 36:1-43 as the introduction to
the remaining narratives in Genesis. We are then able to recognize a design of parallel genealogical structure extending from
Gen 11:10 to 50:26. The rationale for emphasizing the importance
of these genealogies, rather than seeing them only as later redac-
tional additions with no intrinsic relationship to the narratives
that surround them, is that in a family setting, the family relationships expressed through a genealogy are the means of establishing
boundaries of lineage—that is, they identify who is an Israelite
and who is not.

   This study, then, distinguishes itself from past Hebrew Bible
scholarship on the subject of genealogy. Scholars have long agreed
with the assessment of M. Noth that genealogies in the so-called
patriarchal history are secondary additions—that is, literary fabri-
cations—that were constructed to link originally independent and

---

5. For example, C. Westermann, *Genesis 1–11* (Minneapolis: Augsburg, 1984)
566. G. von Rad, however, argues that the break does not come until after 12:1-
9, which was created as a transitional unit between primeval and patriarchal
history; see von Rad, *Genesis* (OTL; Philadelphia: Westminster, 1972) 163. Like
von Rad, U. Cassuto also breaks with scholarly consensus. However, the latter
views Gen 11:10-31 as a unit; see U. Cassuto, *A Commentary on the Book of Genesis*
(Jerusalem: Magnes, 1964) 2.250. Although Coats develops a different structural
design than the one argued for here, he considers the Shem genealogy to have
a structural function in its present position that connects it with what follows
(*Genesis*, 18, 30).

unrelated narrative figures.[6] I am arguing that we must rethink the importance of genealogy in Genesis. Unlike Noth, I believe we do better when we understand that genealogy has a primary literary function within the text. The flow of the narrative units takes its meaning as a resolution to the problem of generational continuity identified within the genealogies. Genealogical progression, accomplished by reproduction, is the aim of any family wishing to perpetuate itself into the next generation. Moving from genealogy (for example, Gen 11:27-32) to stories about family reproduction (Gen 12:1—25:11) back again to genealogy (Gen 25:12-26) is one way for literature to express the passage from generation to generation. Thus, the rationale for arguing that genealogy is primary, and for connecting genealogy and narrative in the family stories of Genesis, would appear to be established not only from a literary

---

6. Following M. Noth (*A History of Pentateuchal Traditions* [Englewood Cliffs, N.J.: Prentice-Hall, 1972] 214-19), M. D. Johnson argues that some of the genealogies of the Pentateuch—and especially those in Genesis conforming to the *Tôlēdōt* formula—function as linking devices between originally independent narratives; see M. D. Johnson, *The Purpose of the Biblical Genealogies* (New York: Cambridge Univ. Press, 1969) 77-82. Johnson's study is concerned with analyzing the literary function of biblical genealogies and was written before biblical scholars began appropriating the insights of anthropologists on the social function of genealogies. See now R. R. Wilson, "The Old Testament Genealogies in Recent Research," *JBL* 94 (1975) 169-89; idem, *Genealogy and History in the Biblical World* (New Haven and London: Yale Univ. Press, 1977). Relying heavily on anthropological evidence for the function of genealogy, Wilson challenges the theory of the origin of genealogy as a linking device between narratives. The questions Wilson puts to the genealogies and their literary context raise different exegetical issues from the ones of concern here. Regardless of the origins of genealogies, I am interested in how they presently interrelate with their narrative surroundings and each other. For the function of the genealogies in Genesis and what historical information they convey, consult T. L. Thompson, *The Historicity of the Patriarchal Narratives: The Quest for the Historical Abraham* (BZAW 133; Berlin: de Gruyter, 1974) 298-314. A discussion of how the Priestly writer gave shape to Genesis through the use of genealogies can be found in F. M. Cross, *Canaanite Myth and Hebrew Epic* (Cambridge, Mass.: Harvard Univ. Press, 1973) 301-5. For a structural analysis of the Genesis genealogies from the perspective of kinship theory, see T. J. Prewitt, "Kinship Structures and the Genesis Genealogies," *JNES* 40 (1981) 87-98. Treatments of the literary importance of pentateuchal genealogies include D. J. A. Clines, *The Theme of the Pentateuch* (JSOTSup 10; Sheffield: JSOT, 1982); M. Fishbane, *Text and Texture: Close Readings of Selected Biblical Texts* (New York: Schocken, 1979) 27-29. Recently J. W. Flanagan has written much from an interdisciplinary perspective on the malleability of genealogies in light of their function in legitimizing social arrangements; see, for example, *David's Social Drama: A Hologram of Israel's Early Iron Age* (The Social World of Biblical Antiquity series 7; Sheffield: Almond, 1988) 193-272.

perspective but also receives support from kinship studies where genealogical links are crucial.[7]

Through the structural analysis of parallel genealogies in Genesis, it becomes possible to discern a shift in perspective from the history of humankind to the history of Israel not at the genealogy of Terah beginning at 11:27, but at the genealogy of Shem beginning at 11:10.[8] The pattern that emerges is as follows: Gen 11:10-26, the genealogy of Shem, is the genealogical prologue, or superscription, that divides primeval history from Israelite history and initiates the first family cycle concerning the sons of Terah. Genesis 11:10-26 is the introduction to the genealogy of Terah in 11:27-32. The latter genealogy is actually the heading for the stories of Terah's sons, Abram, Nahor, and Haran, and their wives, but particularly Abraham and Sarah. The second genealogical cycle opens at Gen 25:12-18;[9] here, the genealogy of Ishmael is the genealogical superscription to the genealogy of Isaac in 25:19-26. The latter genealogy is the introduction to the stories of Isaac's sons and their wives, with special emphasis on Jacob, Rachel, and Leah. The prologue to the final cycle occurs in 36:1-43 with the genealogical superscription concerning the descendants of Esau.

---

7. In support of this argument, see R. A. Oden, "Jacob as Father, Husband, and Nephew: Kinship Studies and the Patriarchal Narratives," *JBL* 102 (1983) 189–205. Oden asserts, "In concentrating instead upon kinship and lineage, one is not only following the present form of the narratives themselves, but also confronting an issue which is dominant in traditional literature generally. Indeed it is artificial to separate traditional literature or mythology from kinship in this regard, since the kinship issues we are following are those recounted in Genesis myths and since it is well established today that both myths and kinship systems are in a sense modes of communication" (193). For the problems posed by Oden's reliance on the alliance theory of Lévi-Strauss, see chapter 1, above.

8. Robinson ("Literary Functions") also notes that the genealogy of Shem begins something new: "At Babel the catastrophic delusion of tower-building alters the shape of the genealogy. Before the tower story the segmented genealogies, which document all the members of each succeeding generation, had seemed simply the natural expression of the mandate to 'be fruitful and multiply.' After the debacle at Babel the genealogies abruptly change form. They become linear, focused as if by the powerful lense of the catastrophe at Babel to trace a single line. The genealogies are no less orderly and no less a continuation of the divine will expressed at creation. But, beginning again with Shem, they do not pause to mark the full extent of human fruitfulness, but march directly to Abraham, the recipient of the promise" (603–4).

9. Silberman argues that the second cycle begins at 22:30 (*sic*) with the mention of the chosen wife, Rebekah, for the true heir, Isaac. This division by Silberman results in the total breakdown in the genealogical structure discerned here; see Silberman, "Listening to the Text," 22.

The genealogy functions as the introduction to the genealogy of Jacob in 37:2. "This is the history/story of the family of Jacob" (Gen 37:2) may be read as an abbreviated form of the stereotypical formula, "These are the generations of...."[10] In the case of the Jacob genealogy the pattern changes and moves directly from "This is the history/story of Jacob" (37:2) to a statement of Joseph's age at the time that the stories of Jacob's sons begin.[11] The genealogy of Jacob may be understood as the introduction to the history of Jacob's sons and his daughter Dinah.

One may therefore conclude that the initial genealogy of each family cycle can function as a superscription, or a prologue, in stereotypical language beginning with the phrase, "This is the history of the family...," and introduces the descendants of Shem (11:10-26), Ishmael (25:12-18), and Esau (36:1-43). These superscriptions prepare the reader for the genealogies of Terah (11:27-32), Isaac (25:19-26), and Jacob (37:2), each of which appears as the introduction to the narratives concerning their offspring and how these offspring beget their own offspring. The latter group of genealogies also uses stereotypical genealogical language. Here again, the phrase "These are the generations of..." marks the beginning of the genealogical unit.

We should not forget that Shem, Ishmael, and Esau are each characters in the narratives that precede their genealogies. For example, the family history of Abraham and Sarah includes stories about Ishmael and his history. Then as the generation of Abraham and Sarah draws to a close and the literature prepares for us to move to the succeeding generation with its focus on the "chosen heir" Isaac, issues about Ishmael's family life need resolution. The Hebrew Bible presents information on the individual who will not be the Israelite lineal heir in the following generation. One may

---

10. See Cross, *Canaanite Myth*, 301–5; M. Fishbane, "Composition and Structure in the Jacob Cycle (Gen 25:19—35:22)," *JJS* 26 (1975) 23 n. 23; reprinted in *Text and Texture*, 40–62; Fisher, "Patriarchal Cycles," 61. None of these authors discerns the structural parallels that result when the genealogy of Shem is seen as the superscription to the genealogy of Terah—instead of as the conclusion to primeval history. Regarding Gen 37:1, see chapter 4 n. 8, below.

11. With the generation of Jacob's twelve sons, there is a switch from linear/vertical to segmented/horizontal genealogy. In chapter 4, below, I discuss the significance of this shift. See K. R. Andriolo, "A Structural Analysis of Genealogy and Worldview in the Old Testament," *American Anthropologist* 75 (1973); and Oden, "Jacob as Father."

argue that the family histories of Shem, Ishmael, and Esau may be found in their genealogies; their genealogies are their stories, albeit in non-narrative form. However, the genealogies of Terah, Isaac, and Jacob function in a different manner. In their cases, each of their genealogies becomes a vehicle for shifting to the narratives that will report their family histories.[12]

An additional rationale for dividing the six genealogies into two groups—Shem, Ishmael, and Esau; Terah, Isaac, and Jacob—is provided when we realize that the genealogies of Shem, Ishmael, and Esau describe the natural flow of family history moving from one generation to the next. A man begets a son who begets his own son, and so the family line is perpetuated into the future. There is a certain monotony to this uninterrupted, uncomplicated record of generational continuity.

In contrast to this stable state of family affairs, the genealogies of Terah, Isaac, and Jacob are marked by situations where there is a problem of heirship. Although the difficulties faced in each of these genealogical cycles differ, and their resolution provides information on various options available in ancient Israel for determining heirship, all three experience some major complication in perpetuating their lineage. At the beginning of the narratives it is not clear what strategy will be used to obtain an heir in the generation following the son or sons fathered by Terah, Isaac, and Jacob.[13] The narratives following the genealogies of Terah, Isaac, and Jacob work out problems found in the genealogies.

The precedent established in Gen 11:10-26 is that a man begets a family, but that only one of his sons is listed as his direct, his lineal or vertical, heir. In the genealogies of Terah, Isaac, and Jacob, a problem of heirship occurs such that it is questionable whether this pattern of progression of descendants can be carried forward.

---

12. See U. Cassuto, *A Commentary on the Book of Genesis* (Jerusalem: Magnes, 1961) 1.99. Although Prewitt's comments pertain to Genesis 4 and 10, his remarks are relevant at this point. He argues one should attend to "the genealogical distinction, citing one blessed line and another beset with curse or difficulty" (*Elusive Covenant*, 6). One notes that the genealogy of Terah beginning in 11:27 includes details concerning Haran's fate before it addresses the situation of Abram.

13. "The name of the plot is 'The True Heir...'" (Silberman, "Listening to the Text," 18). See also Fishbane ("Composition and Structure," 37) and Fisher ("Patriarchal Cycles," 61–62) for differing attempts to define the thematic unity in these narratives.

In the genealogy concerning Terah, Gen 11:30 reports—at a point
seemingly out of place by the standards of 11:10-26, where there
is constant genealogical succession, but proleptic to the ensuing
stories—that Abram's wife, Sarai, is barren.[14] The author in this
way informs readers about the family crisis facing Abram's lineage. More specifically, this information provides the focus for the
attempts at determining an heir that will characterize the entire
group of narratives following the Terah genealogy. As we read
through these stories we discover the various alternatives Abram
utilizes so that his father's lineage can progress and another generational cycle can begin.[15] The fates of the other sons mentioned in
Terah's genealogy, Nahor and Haran, are secondary kinship concerns in the narratives of 12:1—25:11. We are provided with some
of their family histories, though most of what we are told is related
to the subject of Sarah's childlessness.

The same relationship between genealogical problem and narrative resolution exists in the other two narrative cycles, those
about Isaac and Jacob. In contrast to the problem of a lack of
an heir facing Abram, in the genealogy found in 25:19-26 regarding Isaac, we are presented with a situation of one too
many potential lineal heirs. Here the narrative focuses on the
two sons, twins, borne to Isaac by Rebekah. In this family cycle, the question of heirship revolves around deciding which of
Isaac's two sons, Jacob or Esau, will serve as the genealogical
link that will move the family lineage forward to the next generation. The structure of the Jacob genealogy is different from
the preceding ones precisely because the narratives that follow
it are concerned with a different sort of family problem—Jacob
has twelve sons (and a daughter), all of whom are legitimate lineal heirs. Since they are borne to Jacob by his two wives Rachel
and Leah, who are sisters (this is of utmost importance), all the
children hold equal status within the family.[16] Moreover, at this
point, the Israelite lineage switches from a linear to a segmented

---

14. Westermann argues that 11:30, "the motif of the childless mother," is actually the beginning of the Abraham narratives (C. Westermann, *The Promises to the
Fathers* [Philadelphia: Fortress, 1980] 133).

15. See L. R. Helyer, "The Separation of Abram and Lot: Its Significance in the
Patriarchal Narratives," *JSOT* 26 (1983) 82.

16. On why the sons of Bilhah and Zilpah are also legitimate heirs to Jacob
along with the sons of Rachel and Leah, see chapter 4, below.

one.[17] As a result of this shift in genealogical reckoning, the Hebrew Bible now follows the story of all twelve descendants of Jacob.

In the prior discussion, I have attempted to demonstrate that the heirship questions introduced in the genealogies of men (namely, Terah, Isaac, and Jacob) depend for their resolution upon matters relating to women (namely, the status of the women, the number of women, and their fertility). Furthermore, decisions on heirship are linked to the diverse marriage arrangements by which the men are joined to the women. Hagar is fertile but is a servant, while Sarai is childless though she is a legal wife (polycoity); Rebekah gives birth to twin sons (monogamy); the sisters Leah and Rachel together bear twelve sons (sororal polygyny). The Genesis narratives address the different, but highly important, problems to heirship that revolve around these women. Therefore, instead of applying the traditional narrative labels (for example, the Abraham cycle), I designate the family cycles by the names of the women whose positions within the family unit are central in working out problems of descent. These characters become pivotal to the family stories in Genesis. Using the genealogical boundaries outlined above, I consider Gen 11:10—25:11 the "Sarah-Hagar cycle"; Gen 25:12—35:29 the "Rebekah cycle"; and Gen 36:1—50:26 the "Rachel-Leah cycle."[18]

The outline entitled "Structural Design of Family Stories" distinguishes between the three genealogical superscriptions of Shem, Ishmael, and Esau and the three genealogies of Terah, Isaac, and Jacob, which introduce the narratives. This division between the two groups of genealogies casts a shadow on the former three individuals. While Shem, Ishmael, and Esau become part of the segmented, extended genealogy of the ancient Near East, the ver-

---

17. Oden ("Jacob as Father") also notes the significance of the shift from linear to segmented genealogy with the birth of Jacob's children, but argues that it occurs because of the importance of marriage to one's mother's brother's daughters.

18. On the first cycle, Westermann notes: "It is quite remarkable that we do not find a group of true Abraham stories, that is, stories in which Abraham really is the focus of events (a point also made by Noth, who arrives at this observation by a different route). When there is a dramatic concentration of the narrative in the Abraham cycle, Abraham is not really central; he may be a spectator or participant, but he is neither the subject nor object of crucial events. The Abraham cycle contains many narratives in which someone is threatened or endangered—but it is never Abraham" (Westermann, *Promises*, 59 n. 36).

STRUCTURAL DESIGN OF FAMILY STORIES

I. THE SARAH-HAGAR CYCLE: POLYCOITY

Genealogical Prologue of Shem (11:10-26)
Genealogy of Terah (11:27-32)

Narrative Resolution (12:1—25:11)

II. THE REBEKAH CYCLE: MONOGAMY

Genealogical Prologue of Ishmael (25:12-18)
Genealogy of Isaac (25:19-26)

Narrative Resolution (25:27—35:29)

III. THE RACHEL-LEAH CYCLE: SORORAL POLYGYNY

Genealogical Prologue of Esau (36:1-43)
Genealogy of Jacob (37:2)

Narrative Resolution (37:3—50:26)

---

tical transmission of the Israelite family line passes through the
genealogies of Terah, Isaac, and Jacob.[19]

Genesis 11:27-32

The genealogical superscription of Shem (11:10-26) is laconic and
monotonous. It records the name of a single man in each generation descended from Shem. In a stereotypical pattern, the reader
learns of the individual's birth, the age when he became a father
and the name of his lineal heir, that the man begat other children

---

19. For a more traditional analysis of the genealogy of Shem, see B. Vawter,
On Genesis: A New Reading (Garden City, N.Y.: Doubleday, 1977) 159–63. Vawter
notes the structural similarities between Genesis 5 and Gen 11:10-26 and argues
that the latter has been consciously shaped to harmonize with the former. Those
who attempt to relate 11:10-26 to 11:27-32 do so on the theory that Abram is
indeed the firstborn of Terah, a fact never made explicit in Genesis. Thus, so the
argument goes, Abram is similar to Shem in that both are the first of three sons
born to a man (Terah and Noah, respectively) who has a genealogy end with him.
Of course, while a new genealogical list begins with Shem, there is no genealogy
of Abraham.

(whose names are not given), and how many years he lived after the birth of his heir. For example, in regard to the descendants of Eber, we are informed of the birth of Peleg when Eber was thirty-four years old (11:16). Verses 18-19 move on to tell us that when Peleg was thirty he fathered Reu and then lived another two hundred and nine years after the birth of this son, during which time other children were born to him. In other words, the genealogy of Shem notes the steady and stable progress of the family line. There are neither interruptions in it nor variations in presentation of genealogical information.

The format of the genealogy of Terah in 11:27-32 stands in sharp contrast. In v. 27, the genealogy of Terah quickly moves on from the father, Terah, to name his three sons, Abram, Nahor, and Haran. Then we are told a bit of information about each of these three sons: Haran died before his father, Terah, but not before fathering Lot (vv. 27-28); Nahor is married to Milcah (v. 29); Abram has a wife named Sarai, but she is barren (vv. 29-30). At this point we learn why Abram will have a problem continuing his father's lineage. Genesis moves from the genealogy of Shem, a genealogical record with no depth, to the genealogy of Terah, which will require exploration of family history. Genesis 11:27 immediately introduces the men whose fates will determine the future of the genealogy of Terah and provide the details for the narratives that follow.

At first glance, the mention of Lot in v. 27 seems unusual amid the list of Terah's sons. After all, Lot is a son of the second, the descending, generation of Terah. The rationale for including Lot in the genealogy at this early point is clarified in 11:28; Lot's father, Haran, died before his own father, Terah, leaving Lot to be his heir in the next generation after Terah. With the notice of this second generation, the genealogy moves back to the men of the first generation of Terah and provides the names of the wives of these men. Then, the reader is informed that Abram's wife is barren.

Genesis 11:30 introduces the problem of heirship that makes questionable the future of Terah's descendants through the line of Abram. The somewhat awkward manner in which Lot's name suddenly occurs in v. 27 and in which the genealogy mentions Sarai's barrenness in v. 30 suggests that the future of the second generation will probably be secured through Lot; Lot will function as the son that Abram will never father through his wife.[20] From comparative kinship studies we learn that adoption is one strategy for heirship in the case of barrenness. The preferential male in such situations—especially in a patrilineal descent line where there is property involved—is the husband's brother's son. In the interest of inheritance of name and property, the husband adopts the closest male within his lineage, namely, his nephew. Adoption of a nephew by his uncle can occur regardless of whether or not the biological father of the nephew is alive.[21] Adoption in the case of childlessness provides the adopter with a lineal heirship; it does not express concern for the welfare of the adoptee.[22]

Genesis 11:31 reports, "Terah took Abram his son and Lot the son of Haran, his grandson, and Sarai his daughter-in-law, his son Abram's wife, and they went forth together from Ur of the Chaldeans to go into the land of Canaan; but when they came to Haran, they settled there." The verse identifies Abram, Lot, and Sarai according to their relationship to Terah. In the list of individuals who accompanied Terah when he left Ur, Abram's name follows Terah's and then is followed by Lot's. One might have expected Sarai's name to have followed her husband's. Had this happened, the genealogy would have progressed through each succeeding generation. Instead, Sarai is mentioned after Lot. The order of names in this verse of the genealogy implies Lot's connection to Abram as putative heir. The genealogy ends at v. 32 with the notice of the death of Terah. The scene now shifts to narratives that will establish whether or not Lot is Abram's vertical

---

20. Silberman, "Listening to the Text," 20, and Helyer, "Separation of Abram and Lot," 80–83.

21. J. Goody, *Production and Reproduction* (Cambridge Studies in Social Anthropology 17; Cambridge: Cambridge Univ. Press, 1976) 66–85 passim, esp. 74–75.

22. Goody identifies three reasons for adoption: "(i) to provide homes for orphans, bastards, foundlings and the children of impaired families; (ii) to provide childless couples with social progeny; (iii) to provide an individual or couple with an heir to their property" (*Production and Reproduction*, 68). To be fair, there is ambiguity in Genesis at this point. Since we do not know Lot's age at the time, it is also possible that Abram is providing Lot with a home when the two travel together. I prefer the idea that Abram is "adopting" Lot for reasons of heirship. This better explains why Lot accompanies Abram, rather than remaining with Nahor in "the old country." It would have been safer for Lot to remain with the known in Haran, rather than travel to parts unseen with Abram. We do not yet know that Nahor has offspring of his own.

heir. These stories work out the future of the descendants of Terah who are responsible for the family's progression from one generation to the next as they deal with the threat that Sarai's barrenness poses to the future of Abram's line.

Before moving ahead, a question remains: Why did Nahor not follow his father when the latter departed from Ur? Is it because this particular son was not to be involved in the future lineage of his own family? As we will see below (in the discussion of Gen 22:20-24; 24), it is precisely because of Nahor's important role in providing a bride, a kinswoman, for the second generation of Terah's family that, for the time being, he is lost to the story and left behind in his father's native land. When surveying the literary design of Gen 12:1—25:11, one discovers that the Bible reports the family history of Nahor only at the point in Abram's story when it becomes relevant. The story eventually relies on Nahor's presence in Ur to conclude the cycle of Terah's descendants. Genesis 22:20-24, a genealogical notice that relates the end of the Sarah-Hagar cycle back to its beginning and tells of Nahor and Milcah's offspring, will account for Nahor and make clear why the narrator originally made no mention of the fecundity of Nahor's wife, Milcah, when she was first introduced in Gen 11:29 along with the barren Sarai.

The genealogy of Terah in 11:27-32 introduces his three sons, Abram, Nahor, and Haran; his grandson Lot; and Sarai and Milcah, the wives of his two living sons. The tradition then focuses on Abram, whose wife Sarai is unable to bear him an heir, and Lot, the nephew who possibly may serve as this heir. Having already seen that genealogical concerns advance the plot of the family stories in Genesis, we can now discern how the narratives in 12:1—25:11 supplement the genealogy of Terah by considering various strategies of heirship to solve the problem posed by Sarai's barrenness.

The author's chief interest in the Sarah-Hagar cycle concerns the question of who Abram's heir will be. Various answers are put forth, but we will soon discover that not just any heir will suffice before the generation of Abram can close and a new generation begin. My discussion of decisions on heirship in this narrative cycle, as with the Rebekah cycle, and the Rachel-Leah cycle, depends upon discerning patterns of heirship in the narratives and then analyzing them in light of comparative kinship data. Such an approach distinguishes between patterns elicited from the texts and rules articulated within them.[23]

Genesis 12:1-9

The first narrative unit in the story of Abram's attempts to determine who his heir will be is 12:1-9. Tied together by verbs of motion, *hālak* (he went), *yāṣā'* (he came forth), *'ābar* (he passed through), *'ataq* (he moved on), and *nāsa'* (he journeyed on), the unit is further knit tightly by the deity's statements instructing Abram to leave Haran and travel to Canaan, where Yahweh leads him. In this passage we learn that the human obediently does just what the deity commands. Yahweh's intentions for Abram's future, given in vv. 1-3, are made clear as the latter journeys toward his unknown goal. God promises to be with Abram, as well as to provide the land, descendants, and blessing.

The report of Abram's obedience to God's call (vv. 4-6) leads to Yahweh's promise that the patriarch will have progeny (v. 7) who will inherit this land. We learn that before Yahweh makes this promise of descendants, Lot accompanies Abram in his travels (v. 4). In the following verse, we are reminded that Sarai is in the company of the two men (v. 5); here her name precedes Lot's. The contrast between the order of individuals in vv. 4 and 5 could imply that Lot has a more important place in Abram's genealogical future and for matters of inheritance than does Sarai. This list may be intended to echo 11:31. Yet, in v. 5, Abram and Sarai are mentioned as a conjugal unit—only then to have the name of Lot follow their own. Verse 5 mentions both Sarai and Lot and defines them through their relationship to Abram, emphasizing the as yet unclear position of this trio as it relates to the search for Abram's heir. The promise of progeny, interspersed with references to the barren Sarai and the fatherless Lot, serves to underscore the fact that at this point in his life Abram has neither biological son nor heir of his own.

When we read this unit in light of two later texts, which also take up the subject of strategies for identifying an heir for Abram, an interesting pattern emerges. The relevant texts are 12:1-9, 15:1-21, and 17:1-27. These texts serve as divine statements of Yahweh's

---

23. Unfortunately, the latter do not exist.

understanding of who Abram's heir will be. In the first of these three texts, 12:1-9, Yahweh is rather vague about the divine plan. Nothing more specific is stated than that Abram will eventually become a great nation and have descendants who will inherit the land. How this will happen is not explained. Given this generality in Yahweh's words, there is no reason to exclude the possibility that Lot will be the one through whom Abram's lineage will grow to the size emphasized in Genesis 12. Adoption of a blood relative, the son of one's brother, allows for the continuation of Abram's lineage. The preferred adoption choice, from the perspective of the lineage, is the closest male kinsman available. Within the kinship sphere, adoption serves the interests of Abram by providing for social reproduction (that is, the continuance of the family line) and by designating someone as heir to property. As noted earlier, this rationale for adoption contrasts with the situation whose intent is to guarantee the welfare of the adopted person, or to provide the couple with social progeny.

At this point in the story, Abram, and the reader, are left to infer from the continued references to Lot, alongside mention of the barren wife Sarai, that special significance is attached to Lot for the future of Abram's genealogical line. An alternative possibility will be suggested only in 15:1-21[24] and then yet another one in 17:1-27 when Yahweh intervenes with a further pronouncement concerning the issue of preferential heirship. For the time being, however, Lot's presence in Abram's life seems to advance the family situation toward the reestablishment of stable genealogical progression last seen in the genealogy of Shem.[25]

Having assessed Lot's genealogical function in Abram's family history, it is appropriate now to comment on his literary character. First, one may view him as a foil for Abram. For example, the story presents a sharp contrast between Lot's character in chapter 13 and Abram's. When the two kinsmen separate, Abram generously allows his nephew to choose where he will live. Lot chooses all the best land, the well-watered land, the land most like the Garden of Eden (vv. 10-11). Further, Lot's departure from his uncle retards

---

24. L. A. Turner, *Announcements of Plot in Genesis* (JSOTSup 96; Sheffield: JSOT, 1990) 62–74, 79–82.

25. For the observation that the narratives of Abraham, Isaac, and Jacob are patterned from a framing device of blessing, see Fishbane, "Composition and Structure," 36.

the action of the promise story and heightens the narrative suspense. If one, properly, assumes Lot to be Abram's future heir, a crisis for the promise results when Lot takes off to work out his own destiny.[26]

Genesis 12:10—13:1

In this episode, Abram attempts to solve the problem that Sarai's barrenness poses for the family. The unit 12:10—13:1 takes Abram and Sarai to Egypt at the time of a famine in the land of Canaan.[27] Like the preceding episode, this one is framed by verbs of motion—the first, *wayyēred*, indicating movement down into Egypt, the second, *wayya'al*, indicating movement up from Egypt. One should include 13:1 as the final verse of this unit because it is conjunctive to the preceding verse while 13:2 begins with a disjunctive clause. Form-critical reasoning corroborates that 12:10—13:1 is a unity and applies to it the genre label "saga," while noting the limited value of such a label for interpreting the text.[28]

In order to appreciate fully the meaning of this narrative, it must be read in context. Abram has a wife, who, so it seems thus far, is incapable of bearing him a child. This is the only detail provided about the marriage of Abram and Sarai up to this point in

---

26. Helyer, "Separation of Abram and Lot."

27. This text and the other two narratives reporting a case of the patriarch passing his wife off as his sister in a foreign land (Genesis 20 and 26) have received much scholarly attention. Analysis is usually based on source assignment and aimed at establishing chronological literary priority. This sort of study has been attempted from every scholarly angle. Still, no consensus has been reached. However, all would concur that Speiser's attempt to explain the "wife-sister" custom on the basis of alleged parallels in the Nuzi texts has not been substantiated by comparative ancient Near Eastern material. See E. A. Speiser, "The Wife-Sister Motif in the Patriarchal Narratives," *Studies and Texts*, vol. 1: *Biblical and Other Studies* (Waltham, Mass.: Philip W. Lown Institute of Advanced Judaic Studies, Brandeis University, 1963) 15–28; reprinted in *Oriental and Biblical Studies* (ed. J. J. Finkelstein and M. Greenberg; Philadelphia: Univ. of Pennsylvania Press, 1969) 62–82. Noteworthy is R. Polzin (" 'The Ancestress of Israel in Danger' in Danger," *Semeia* 3 [1975] 81–98) for his illustration of the possibilities for new narrative meaning that result when much-studied texts are analyzed synchronically rather than diachronically. One work that interrelates these stories in Genesis to others outside this context is P. Miscall, "Literary Unity in Old Testament Narrative," *Semeia* 15 (1979) 27–44.

28. For a summary of scholarship on form-criticism and the wife-sister texts, consult D. L. Petersen, "A Thrice-Told Tale: Genre, Theme and Motif," *BR* 18 (1973) 30–43.

Genesis. The two would appear to be defined solely on the basis of status: husband and barren wife.[29] And as indicated earlier, the latter status poses a problem for a household concerned to have an heir. A woman who is barren would seem to be of little functional significance to her husband under such circumstances; she has not fulfilled her role in a family and a society interested in progeny.

Abram finds himself in a foreign land where he stands to gain much through the beauty of the woman who is unable to fulfill her primary biological function of providing an heir for the family lineage. We are told how Abram took charge of this situation and commanded his wife to call herself his sister.[30] The story tersely narrates the ensuing events. Once the couple reaches their destination, the Egyptian officials spot the beautiful woman, and as a result of their praise the pharaoh desires her. Nothing is said of Sarai's reaction to what happens to her. We hear Abram's words to her (vv. 11-13) and pharaoh's words about her to Abram (18-19), but never Sarai's words or even her thoughts on how the men treat her. May one infer that once Abram tells Sarai to pretend she is his sister, she does so with no suggestion of resistance on her part?[31] On the basis of cross-cultural studies on childless wives, it appears that, due to her barrenness, Sarai can react in no other way.[32]

Genesis 12:18-19 suggests that Sarai had no power to resist when confronted by pharaoh's men. Only Abram is indicted for

---

29. Not without significance, the word 'iššâ occurs eleven times in this unit. Sarai is both primary wife and woman, yet she is never said to be the one whom Abram is said to love, as he is said to love Isaac in Genesis 22.

30. I would argue that Abram knows exactly what he is doing here in terms of Sarai and the wealth he will acquire in exchange for her. On this basis, Petersen's reference to "Abraham's conflicting feelings" seems unsubstantiated (Petersen, "Thrice-Told Tale," 36).

31. Westermann (Genesis 12–36 [Minneapolis: Augsburg, 1985] 163) sees vv. 11-13 as a dialogue between Abram and Sarai. He says, "The speech shows that it is a matter of dialog even though there is no answer from Sarah. It is part of narrative technique that the answer can be left out where silence suffices; it indicates that Sarah agrees." This literary judgment fails to explain why Sarai would go along with such a plan.

32. The precarious plight of a woman without a child for her husband's lineage is a familiar topic in sociological and anthropological literature on patrilineal societies. For information on the connection between a woman's power and her record in childbearing, see J. F. Collier, "Women in Politics," Woman, Culture, and Society (ed. M. Z. Rosaldo and L. Lamphere; Stanford, Calif.: Stanford Univ. Press, 1974) 89–96; and E. A. Michaelson and W. Goldschmidt, "Female Roles and Male Dominance among Peasants," Southwestern Journal of Anthropology 27 (1971) 330–52.

having dissembled about his relationship to Sarai. Because Abram lied when he said that Sarai was his sister, Sarai moves from the company of her husband, Abram, into the home of a stranger, the pharaoh of Egypt. Interpreting the episode of Abram, Sarai, and pharaoh from a cross-disciplinary perspective, it appears that Abram is motivated by a desire to overcome the obstacle that Sarai's barrenness presents to his chance to father a biological heir. He will remove her from the family. Abram is maneuvering to be rid of Sarai so that he can get another wife for himself.[33] However, literary analysis understands the pericope as the first of many crises to the divine promise made to Abram in chapter 12.[34] Without a wife—even a barren one—how can Abram expect the realization of the promise that he will be a great nation (12:2)? Living within the confines of pharaoh's home, Sarai can hardly bear Abram his promised son.

One may ask whether survival issues motivate Abram. Either he loses Sarai or he loses his life. True as that may seem, let us jump ahead briefly to the final so-called wife-sister text, Gen 26:1-33. In this story similar circumstances prevail (a famine, a foreign setting, a fear of death because the local men want the Israelite woman), but with different results. Rebekah never becomes separated from Isaac, and neither of their lives is ever endangered.[35] Therefore, the interpreter must look for a different meaning in the story. The great wealth that pharaoh gives to Abram in exchange for "his sister" may further help us appreciate what is presupposed in this social situation. As we will see, all the marriages

---

33. Contrast the interpretation given by J. H. Otwell: "It seems quite probable that the thrice-told story is a theological statement about the faithfulness of God in covenantal promises rather than a description of a husband's rights over his wife, and that the faithfulness of the Lord is underscored by telling about it in a context in which the patriarchs themselves had acted reprehensively" (J. H. Otwell, *And Sarah Laughed: The Status of Women in the Old Testament* [Philadelphia: Westminster, 1977] 79).

34. Helyer, "Separation of Abram and Lot," 82. Thompson (*Historicity*, 246), who relies on Coats ("Despoiling the Egyptians," *VT* 18 [1968] 450–57), provides a different literary perspective. He posits, "The basic motif is that of 'Despoiling the Egyptians,' which motif affects the treatment of every detail of the story."

35. A complete analysis of this narrative is found in the following chapter. I disagree with Westermann, and other scholars, who argue that the wife-sister texts are three variants of the same story (*Genesis 12–36*, 161). Rather, they are three narratives employing the wife-sister motif to tell three different stories (Petersen, "Thrice-Told Tale," 43). The differences between them are intentional.

arranged in Genesis involve some transfer of material goods from
the groom and his family to the bride and her family. Thus, based
on comparative kinship data, it appears that Abram may be interested in being rid of his barren wife in order to receive property
for her that he will later be able to use to secure another, presumably fertile, wife. One wonders, though, whether the option
of divorce was available to Abram if in fact he was interested in
removing Sarai from the family. If we assume that divorce was a
means of dissolving a marriage, we will need to consider below
why Abram did not resort to such a plan.

Finally, how are we to evaluate the eleven references to Sarai
as woman/wife in this one unit? It seems plausible that this repetition calls attention to the very reason why Abram's attempt
to remove Sarai will never work. The story presupposes 11:29,
the genealogical notice that Sarai is Abram's legal wife; this is the
state of the nuclear family—husband and wife. Certain status and
rights are attached to such a legal arrangement. It would seem
that Yahweh has plagued pharaoh and his household, with the result that Sarai returns to Abram, for exactly the reason mentioned
in v. 17—namely, Sarai is Abram's lawful wife. This is the basis
for their monogamous relationship, although Sarai's role as wife
appears to require that she not be barren.

Thus, the point of the course of action may not be so much that
Sarai per se must be saved; rather, it is a statement about the way
nuclear family units should be maintained. Husband and wife are
meant to stay together in ancient Israel based on their conjugal status.[36] Therefore, Abram's attempt, through illicit human means, to
resolve the heirship problem in his family seems to have met with
negative sanctions. Mention of Lot in the final verse (13:1), after
Sarai and Abram are reunited, suggests that Abram's nephew is
still a good enough answer to the gnawing concern for an heir and
the resolution of inheritance that the topic of Sarai's barrenness
can be put aside.

---

36. See Petersen ("Thrice-Told Tale," 38) on the theme of this pericope. Silberman argues that it was because Sarai per se was Yahweh's choice as mother of
Abram's child that she was returned from pharaoh's house. Contra Silberman, the
text is ambiguous about whether pharaoh did or did not have sexual intercourse
with Sarai (Silberman, "Listening to the Text," 20).

Genesis 13:2-18

No sooner does the narrative appear to affirm Lot's existence as heir apparent to Abram's family than an episode occurs in which the uncle and his nephew separate from each other, each to work out his own fate in resolving kinship issues. Like the two stories that precede it, this narrative is framed by verbs of motion: it begins (after mention of Abram's wealth) when Abram journeys from the Negeb to Bethel (v. 3) and concludes when he moves with his tent to Hebron (v. 18). The boundaries of the pericope are determined by the framework of travel. Between these verses Lot moves his home from inside of Canaan to outside of it.

The story reports on how Abram's and Lot's respective wealth and property become such that each man must live in a geographically separate region—Abram lives in Canaan but Lot does not[37]—thereby spreading the patrilineal descent group of Terah over a larger area than before. More importantly, because Lot is outside of Canaan, he can no longer be lineal descendant to Abram—according to Gen 12:7, Abram's descendants are to be given Canaan. Once Lot no longer resides in Canaan, the one item missing from Abram's wealth, an heir, is now seemingly out of Abram's grasp forever—assuming, of course, that the strategy of adopting the closest kinsman possible, his brother's son, was an option Abram was considering.[38] The significance of this separation is clear from both literary and social-scientific analysis. On the one hand, the departure of Lot causes literary suspense: it threatens the fulfillment of the promise of an heir for Abram. On the other hand, comparative data focus our attention on the fact that Abram and Lot separate because an excess of material possessions makes it impossible for both of them to dwell together. Specifically, they each have so much cattle that there was not enough land for

---

37. See Gen 36:7 and the plight of Jacob and Esau. In Genesis 34 Jacob and Hamor make a treaty to live together with the mutual sharing of property—though both parties already appear to be wealthy. Conflict over property and wealth appears throughout the Genesis stories; it should be noted that men are always the ones involved in this type of conflict.

38. Mesopotamian law codes suggest that in the case of childless couples, an adopted son could serve as legal heir. In Gen 12:4, 5; 13:1, 5, there is much emphasis placed by the narrator on the close relationship between Abram and Lot. But the text never suggests that this relationship has been formalized by adoption procedures. See G. R. Driver and J. C. Miles, *The Babylonian Laws* (2 vols.; Oxford: Clarendon, 1952–1955) 2.75–76 (laws 185–93); 1.388–405.

them (v. 6). Then, the arguments of the employees of these two men directly affect their employers and, most importantly, have repercussions for Abram's kinship relationships.[39] Issues of property and conflict between Abram's and Lot's shepherds provide the focal point for Gen 13:2-18, a text that dramatically advances the plot of the Sarah-Hagar cycle.[40]

Abram insists that the two kin separate so that strife does not divide them (vv. 8-9a). Abram allows Lot first choice in deciding which part of the land he would prefer to dwell in (v. 9b). Lot chooses land outside of Canaan, while Abram remains in Canaan (vv. 10-12). Based on comparative kinship studies of land inheritance patterns we realize that once Lot departs from Canaan and dwells on his own land, he cannot be Abram's designated heir. He must reside on his (adopted) father's land in order to inherit it. Yet the episode is not finished until Abram is assured by Yahweh that an even greater area of land than the one Lot has chosen will belong to Abram's descendants in the future (vv. 14-17). Ironically, no sooner does his presumed heir depart in search of a

39. "Women have families, men have fields" (R. R. Reiter, "Men and Women in the South of France," *Toward an Anthropology of Women* [ed. R. R. Reiter; New York and London: Monthly Review, 1975] 267). So, as noted, in Genesis, strife between men concerns wealth and property while the strife between women concerns husbands and children. In the case of Lot, he buys his autonomy as a result of this strife at the price of having to move to land not properly reckoned as part of Canaan. While Speiser had argued that the issue here is the general settlement in the promised land, Helyer refines this theory when he demonstrates that this land chosen by Lot is not part of Canaan (E. A. Speiser, *Genesis* [AB; Garden City, N.J.: Doubleday, 1964] 97; Helyer, "Separation of Abram and Lot," 80). Vawter makes this same point (*On Genesis*, 185). Thus, the text of Genesis 13 suggests that Lot is no longer a contender for the primary spot in Abram's lineage when he leaves for new parts. The narratives in Genesis appear to presuppose a family situation whereby land is inherited from father to son; men inheriting from each other must live together. Presumably this explains Abraham's insistence in Genesis 24 that at all costs Isaac must not return to Paddan-aram, and Jacob's return to Isaac after dwelling with Laban (Genesis 31–33). On patrilineal inheritance and its effect on gender roles, see Michaelson and Goldschmidt, "Female Roles."

40. On the importance of this text for the advancement of the plot of an heir for Abram and Sarai, see Silberman, "Listening to the Text," 20; and Helyer, "Separation of Abram and Lot," 77–88. A summary of past interpretation of Genesis 13, complete with bibliography, can conveniently be found in Helyer ("Separation of Abram and Lot," 77–79). He notes that these past studies traditionally have seen this chapter as a depiction of (1) Abram the man of faith; (2) the process of settlement in the promised land of Canaan; or (3) the selfishness of Lot in his choice of land. But Helyer correctly notes that all three of these themes are secondary to the crisis that results when Abram's heir apparent, Lot, separates from him.

life of his own than Abram receives a divine guarantee of innumerable descendants. The situation of separation heightens the tension of the plot of heirship to Abram's lineage that is the focus of 11:27—25:11. Who will this heir be?

With the episode in Gen 13:2-18, the subplot of the Sarah-Hagar cycle, the story of Lot's life, begins. As with the other main characters introduced in the genealogy of Terah in 11:27-32, the story of Lot and his descendants will be recounted and resolved before the Sarah-Hagar cycle ends in Genesis 25. We will learn how each of these individuals arranges for an heir in the descending generation. The fate of Lot is a subplot that supplements and provides clues for interpreting the main plot of the Sarah-Hagar cycle.[41] Characterized by tales of territorial strife, war, and destruction, the story of Lot's independent life begins here. This pericope, through its mention of Zoar in v. 10, anticipates the conclusion of the Lot stories in Genesis 19 when Lot is anxious to escape for safety to Zoar.[42]

Genesis 14:1-24

The mention of Zoar in Gen 13:10 strongly suggests that the episode of 13:2-18 must be interpreted with 14:1-24 and that the latter must be analyzed in connection with the narrative subplot of Lot's fate. Zoar is mentioned in Gen 11:27—25:11 only in stories regarding Lot. Chapter 14 serves as the link between the preceding unit and chapter 19, where there are further details of Lot and his life with his neighbors. Here in Gen 14:1-24 we begin to get a glimpse of how Lot fared after he separated from Abram and left Canaan, and we begin to understand how kinship responsibilities affect family life.

The mention of Zoar as early as 14:2 prepares the reader for the fact that in the midst of this story of the war waged by Amraphel, Arioch, Chedorlaomer, and Tidal, the four kings of the East, the focus will narrow down to Lot's involvement in the situation—just as earlier the genealogies of Shem and Terah are the context for the life of Abram. The story moves from the political, a war, to

---

41. Von Rad, *Genesis*, 225; Coats, *Genesis*, 113.

42. For a tradition-historical analysis of the Lot narratives, see R. Kilian, "Zur Überlieferungsgeschichte Lots," *BZ*, NF 14 (1970) 23–37, and the discussion in Noth, *Pentateuchal Traditions*, 151–54.

the personal, Lot as a prisoner of war. What starts out as political ends up as personal. A further link between Lot's story and the story of the war occurs with the notice in 13:12 that Lot moved his tent "as far as Sodom," and the fact that Sodom is one city the four kings attack.[43] The place names, Zoar and Sodom, link chapters 13 and 14 as stories of events in the lives of Abram and Lot; the second story presupposes the first.

This episode of the wars of the kings of the East is, on one level, the first indication of how Lot's fate works out; it tells us how poorly he does in getting settled in his new surroundings. After his active role in choosing to dwell near Sodom (13:12), Lot remains passive (14:16) about the war of the kings. Hence, it would seem that this text fits within the framework of the Lot narratives; despite difficulties in interpretation, we should try to understand it in its present final context. There is no reason to resort to theories connecting it to a level of obscure traditions of Abram's belligerent nature.[44] Although Lot dies to the main plot of the Sarah-Hagar cycle once he separates from Abram, Lot as a kinsman of Abram has his own genealogical fate. Despite the political conditions amid which Lot lives, the narrative suggests that, for the time being, Lot has a new home.[45] As we shall see in Gen 19:30-38, place of residence is linked with genealogy.

---

43. Coats, *Genesis*, 113–14.

44. For example, Y. Muffs asserts, "In short, we have seen that each element of the laws of war found in Genesis 14 has its exact parallel in good ancient Near Eastern tradition. This would seem to make Abraham not merely a pious man but a noble warrior and a politically astute maker of treaties" (Y. Muffs, "Abraham the Noble Warrior: Patriarchal Politics and Laws of War in Ancient Israel," *JJS* 33 [1982] 81–107). One interpretation frequently expressed at present is that Genesis 14 mirrors and anticipates the monarchy—that is, Abraham is understood to be functioning as the military-political prototype of David; see R. E. Clements, *Abraham and David: Genesis 15 and Its Meaning for Israelite Tradition* (SBT 2/5; Naperville, Ill.: Alec R. Allenson, 1967). However, Westermann concludes that in its final (composite) form, the text dates "from the late postexilic period" (Westermann, *Genesis 12–36*, 193).

45. Silberman contends that this unit retards the movement of the plot of the Abraham narratives. He connects the story to the larger body of narratives through the encounter between Abram and the king of Sodom in 14:21-24. Less plausible is his assertion, "Abram's renunciation of spoil suggests that the true heir is to receive nothing that is not part of the divine gift. His inheritance is not to be commingled with anything else" (Silberman, "Listening to the Text," 20). It is difficult to understand how Silberman can suggest this after we have just read in 12:16 of the huge amount of wealth that Abram *willingly* accepted in exchange for Sarai. The wealth that accrued to Abram from pharaoh seemingly did not trouble his conscience.

Comparative data suggest that in some situations, kinship relationships carry with them political functions.[46] In a time of crisis, such as when Lot is taken hostage during war, Abram is expected to aid his nephew. In fact, not only does Abram liberate Lot, but he also frees other war prisoners (v. 16).[47] Finally, chapter 14 foreshadows Abraham's intercessory role in chapter 18 when he bargains with Yahweh over the fate of Sodom and Gomorrah in order to spare the lives of his nephew Lot and Lot's family.[48] These two narratives report on the more political aspects of kinship bonds.

Genesis 15:1-21

The next attempt to designate an heir for Abram—whose future lineage is still threatened by Sarai's barrenness—is recounted in 15:1-21.[49] The narrative incorporates the promise theme that began in Gen 12:1-4. Genesis 15 presents Yahweh's promise of a son (v. 4), the promise of an increase in the number of Abram's descendants until they are as many as the stars in heaven (vv. 5-6), the promise of land (vv. 18-21), and an explanation of why the land promise will not be fulfilled for several generations (vv. 12-16). Alternatively, the text provides further information on strategies

46. R. T. Antoun, *Arab Village: A Social Structural Study of a Transjordanian Peasant Community* (Bloomington: Indiana Univ. Press, 1972) 77.

47. Westermann believes vv. 12-17 and 21-24 derive from premonarchical times, from the so-called period of the judges. He explains why Abram declined the spoils of war: "Charismatic leaders do not want power and wealth for themselves; it is this same attitude that leads Gideon to refuse the kingly honor. The saviors of Israel have no need of a dynasty" (*Genesis 12–36*, 202). I am unable to add anything new to the discussion of Melchizedek's presence in this story. Again, consult Westermann, *Genesis 12–36*, 203–8.

48. Von Rad (*Genesis*, 225) connects chapters 13, 18, and 19 as a narrative unity about Abraham and Lot; Coats (*Genesis*, 114, 119–21) concurs but also includes Genesis 14.

49. Study of this passage with special attention to issues of unity and diversity of sources can be found in J. van Seters, *Abraham in History and Tradition* (New Haven: Yale Univ. Press, 1975) 249–78. For discussion of the covenant between Abram and Yahweh, see Clements, *Abraham and David*; O. Kaiser, "Traditionsgeschichtliche Untersuchung von Genesis 15," *ZAW* 70 (1958) 107–26; S. E. Loewenstamm, "The Divine Grants of Land to the Patriarchs," *JAOS* 91 (1971) 509–10; L. A. Snijders, "Genesis 15: The Covenant with Abraham," *OTS* 12 (1958) 261–79; M. Weinfeld, "The Covenant of Grant in the Old Testament and the Ancient Near East," *JAOS* 90 (1970) 184–203.

of heirship. In this case, Abram sees the possibility of an heir for himself in the person of Eliezer (vv. 2-3), an individual thought to be a servant in his household.[50] The strategy for heirship and social reproduction would now be the adoption of a nonkinsman. However, Yahweh immediately rejects Abram's plan and stipulates that only his own biological son can function as his heir (v. 4).

The episode advances the plot of an heir for Abram by narrowing down the pool of potential candidates suggested in 12:1-9. There Abram was told he would have descendants; seemingly any heir would do. First Abram considers the strategy of adopting a near kinsman; then he suggests the alternative of adopting a nonrelative. But Yahweh provides further information on heirship and indicates that not just anyone will suffice; Abram must be the biological father of his heir. Yahweh specifies the type of child who may be properly reckoned as Abram's heir. Divine statements deliberately and effectively limit the range of speculation on the question of progeny.

Genesis 16:1-15

Genesis 15 supplements our knowledge of options available to a man in ancient Israel for determining his heir apparent, and advances the Sarah-Hagar cycle to 16:1-15, where a son is finally born to Abram. Having already told of two failed attempts by Abram to name an heir, that is, Lot and Eliezer, family history shifts to Sarai and her proposal for resolving the problem presented by her infertility. Sarai means for her maid Hagar to bear Abram an heir. Based on Yahweh's words to Abram mandating that his biological son be his heir (15:1-21), it appears that Sarai's plan will meet with divine sanction. Abram will have a suitable heir[51] from his union

---

50. The question of v. 2 and Eliezer's identity still awaits an answer; various possibilities have been considered. See A. Caquot, "L'alliance avec Abram (Genèse 15)," *Sem* 12 (1962) 57–58; H. Cazelles, "Connexions et structure de Gen. XV," *RB* 69 (1962) 321–49; Clements, *Abraham and David*, 18; H. L. Ginsberg, "Abram's 'Damascene' Steward," *BASOR* 200 (1970) 31–32; H. Seebass, "Gen. 15, 2b," *ZAW* 75 (1963) 317–19; Speiser, *Genesis*, 111–12.

51. Some have turned to ancient Near Eastern legal procedures to explain and justify Sarai's plan. See C. H. Gordon, "Biblical Customs and the Nuzi Tablets," *BA* 3 (1940) 2–3; Speiser, *Genesis*, 119–21; J. van Seters, "The Problem of Childlessness in Near Eastern Law and the Patriarchs of Israel," *JBL* 87 (1968) 401.

with a woman besides Sarai herself. A woman of lesser status, the Egyptian handmaid Hagar, will function as a secondary wife to provide an heir for the family. This option for heirship, which is consistent with the practice of concubinage, sets the stage for the birth of Ishmael as the solution to the problem of generational continuity.

The episode in 16:1-15 begins with a disjunctive clause that has Sarai as its subject, not, as might have been expected, Abram. The first verse provides two seemingly unrelated pieces of information whose relevance is soon explained. Sarai is barren; she has an Egyptian maid named Hagar. Next we learn of Sarai's desire for a child who will serve some purpose in life ("I will be built up from it") rather than solely providing Abram with an heir.[52] In 16:2 Sarai speaks her first direct words, and they convey her determination to have a child. Sarai is as concerned as Abram about progeny. Hagar becomes a substitute for Sarai as the mother of Abram's child; however, comparative evidence informs us that, in such cases, the status of the child will be different from the status of his mother.[53] The child functions as the offspring and heir to the marriage of Abram and Sarai.

Genesis 16 portrays the family situation through the eyes of Sarai and allows us to conclude that pregnancy confers prestige

---

Thompson (*Historicity*, 252–69) rejects the argument that Sarai's act of giving Hagar to Abram is a strict reflection of second-millennium (or seventh century, so van Seters) legal and social customs. Thompson believes the cuneiform documents suggest personal choice in this situation, rather than "codified law or even necessarily custom" (259). Consult Thompson for the relevant Near Eastern documents.

52. Given the determination Sarai shows here and elsewhere, Noth's tradition-historical conclusions are unconvincing. In arguing that Sarai is difficult to think of as a developed narrative figure, he says, "Even more colorless than Rebekah alongside of Isaac appears Sarah at the side of Abraham. Actually she is thought of only for her dignity as the wife of Abraham and the mother of the heir promised to him. Her name clearly means 'mistress, gentlewoman.' Like the figure Sarah, the name itself is a construct created for the purpose of the Abraham narratives and as such is overshadowed by the figure and the portrayal of Abraham. No more than any of the other female figures of the 'patriarchal' history is she an independent subject of tradition" (Noth, *Pentateuchal Traditions*, 151). Maybe Noth's opinion would make Sarah laugh as much as the news she received in Gen 18:2 did! See also S. E. McEvenue, "A Comparison of Narrative Styles in the Hagar Stories," *Semeia* 3 (1975) 64–80.

53. "If a man had no child by a wife, the child of his concubine inherited his status, position, and occupation as well" (Goody, *Production and Reproduction*, 47).

on a woman in ancient Israel.[54] The text specifically reports that
once Hagar learned of her pregnancy, she looked down on her
barren mistress (v. 4: *watttēqal gebirtâh be'ênêhā*). Despite the fact
of Hagar's servitude, her status in the family has been increased
by her pregnancy.[55] Ultimately, of course, this situation becomes
threatening to the barren Sarai, and she expels the pregnant
Hagar.[56]

This pericope exposes fierce competition between the two

Goody's study contains many examples from the Bible, which he considers to
replicate the social situation in ancient Israel. Goody specifically refers to Genesis
16 and notes that a woman's servant can legitimately serve as a surrogate mother
in providing an heir to a barren woman and her husband (48). Hagar functions as
a slave wife to Abram for purposes of procreation. Goody also maintains that the
legal wife might bring such a servant to her marriage as part of her dowry. The
Bible provides us with no information on when and where Sarai acquired Hagar.
Although Hagar's Egyptian background raises the possibility that she may have
been included in the gifts pharaoh gave Abram in Genesis 12, it is just as likely
that she was included in Sarah's dowry. It would not appear that "the woman
of the house" was automatically in charge of maidservants and "the man of the
house" was automatically in charge of menservants. I make this judgment based
on Gen 12:16, where Abram receives gifts from pharaoh, including maidservants,
while Sarai is in pharaoh's home. At that stage in the story, Abram is without a
woman of the house.

54. For an analysis of the family situation based on the theory that in patri-
lineally organized households the interests of husbands and wives do not coincide
with each other and result in domestic disharmony, see B. S. Denich, "Sex and
Power in the Balkans," *Woman, Culture, and Society* (ed. M. Z. Rosaldo and
L. Lamphere; Stanford, Calif.: Stanford Univ. Press, 1974) 243–62.

55. This change in status appears to be reflected in adjectives describing Hagar. She is first described as Sarah's *šipḥâ* (maidservant/female slave), but after
bearing a son she is called an *'āmâ* (handmaid/concubine/slave wife). The former appears to reflect a lower status than the latter term according to A. Berlin,
Poetics and Interpretation of Biblical Narrative (Bible and Literature series; Sheffield:
Almond, 1983) 88, 152. I think there is a danger in being too literal in translating
either of these two terms. Terms used in social anthropology, such as *concubine*
and *slave wife*, appear applicable in Hagar's case, despite the fact that these are not
traditionally the translations of the two Hebrew words above. All of these terms
can be applied to a woman who is a secondary wife, which is the way Goody
understands Hagar. Genesis 16:3 indicates that Sarai gave Hagar to Abram to be
his *'iššâ*.

56. J. A. Hackett studies the power relationship between Sarah and Hagar
in light of a narrative pattern discerned in texts from Mesopotamia and Ugarit
and offers a critique of Sarah's treatment of Hagar. She argues that Hagar is the
heroine of the story and that the reader is expected to sympathize with her as
an abused individual; see J. A. Hackett, "Rehabilitating Hagar: Fragments of an
Epic Pattern," *Gender and Difference in Ancient Israel* (ed. P. L. Day; Minneapolis:
Fortress, 1989) 12–27.

women.[57] Although we have no direct evidence that Sarai brought
economic goods to the marriage,[58] such is the case with other matriarchs in Genesis. On the one hand, it is possible to argue that
because Sarai is Abram's primary wife and cannot be divorced
because he would lose economic goods, Sarai occupies a higher
social position than her servant, who is Abram's secondary wife.
All the same, Sarai's barrenness brings a psychological advantage
to the maidservant, once the latter becomes pregnant by Sarai's
husband. One might imagine a situation where Sarai and Hagar
band together to have some advantage against Abram, but the
opposite happens here.[59]

On the other hand, it is unnecessary to divorce a barren
woman—even if she brought no dowry to the marriage fund—in
societies that allow polycoity (concubines) or polygyny (additional wives). A man with a barren wife may simply take an
additional wife. In such cases, competition between women typically results. The intense rivalry between Sarai and Hagar is
expressed by Sarai's intolerance of Hagar's haughtiness. Sarai is
jealous. Although one might argue that this jealousy is a characteristic of Sarai's personality, from a cross-cultural perspective,
jealousy and being a co-wife go hand in hand.[60] This jealousy may
account for the situation that at no time in the story do the two
women speak directly to each other. Abram serves as their intermediary. Sarai works to control the conditions in her life by
expelling Hagar, but she effects this change only after appealing

57. Having noted the significance of women's quarrels in the domestic realm,
Westermann treats this narrative chiefly in terms of the promise theme which he
argues ties the larger context of the family stories together (*Promises*, 63-64). One
wonders why Westermann is so quick to move beyond this first and original layer
of meaning to larger thematic questions. The issue of chapter 16 is the relative
social positions of the two women; their antagonism toward each other is the
basis for all events that occur here and in Genesis 21. See the similar assessment
of the centrality of the women's quarrels in Coats's review of Westermann, *JBL*
101 (1982) 280.

58. R. Westbrook considers the possibility that Hagar may have been part of
Sarah's dowry (*Property and the Family in Biblical Law* [JSOTSup 113; Sheffield:
JSOT Press, 1991] 145).

59. For two important studies, arguing that women's quarrels are their way
of exercising power by calling attention to their opinions and thereby affecting
decisions, see J. F. Collier, "Women in Politics," and Denich, "Sex and Power."
When it serves their mutual interests, women band together; when it does not,
they do not.

60. Goody, *Production and Reproduction*, 42-43.

to Abram;[61] however, v. 6 is unclear and we cannot be certain whether Abram gives Sarai permission to do what she desires to Hagar—based on his authority as head of the household—or whether he is chiding her for not acting on what is legitimately within her right as primary wife and as mistress of a slave.[62] It is only because of the status differential between them that Sarah can expel Hagar. In the case of equal co-wives (that is, sororal polygyny), such as Rachel and Leah, such action would not be sanctioned.

In Gen 16:1-15, as in 12:10—13:1, Sarai and Abram relate on the basis of status—barren wife and husband—yet the primacy of the conjugal unit is maintained. Although Hagar provides Abram with his long-awaited child, she lives in a situation of subordination to Sarai, her mistress. Sarai retains her status as first wife in Abram's household; Hagar maintains her position as secondary wife but as mother of Abram's child. The issue that requires resolution in chapter 16 is the relative social positions of the two women; their antagonism toward each other is the basis for all the events that occur here. Moreover, these antagonisms foreshadow what will happen in Genesis 21.

Genesis 15:1-21 states that a child fathered by Abram could serve as his heir, making it seem that with the birth of Ishmael in 16:15, Sarai's barrenness no longer is an impediment to the continuation of the family line. Indeed, 16:1-15 ends on the happy note of Ishmael's birth. At this point in the narrative, Abram is eighty-six years old.

Genesis 17:1-27

While information on Abram's age ends Genesis 16, the subject reappears at the beginning of chapter 17. Thirteen years have

---

61. See the situation of Rebekah and Isaac in Genesis 27; the wife's plan to switch the birth order of the two sons needs the blessing of her husband.

62. "Divide and conquer" would appear to be Abram's policy in dealing with the potentially explosive strife between Sarai and Hagar. On the power of women's words and the politics of gossip, see S. Harding, "Women and Words in a Spanish Village," *Toward an Anthropology of Women* (ed. R. R. Reiter; New York and London: Monthly Review, 1975) 283–308. Since there are so few instances in biblical literature of women interacting with each other, what little evidence we do have must be thoroughly considered in order better to comprehend how women and men functioned in Israelite society.

passed, making Abram ninety-nine years old when we resume his family story. From the subject of age in v. 1 we move quickly to a new topic, a covenant, in v. 2. By means of the covenant of circumcision with Abram,[63] Yahweh initially seems to confirm Ishmael as Abram's heir. The change of name from Abram to Abraham, "father of a multitude," suggests divine confirmation that, through the birth of Ishmael, Abraham's descent line will be secured. In form, the episode is chiefly a divine soliloquy telling Abraham of all that will be done for him if he will circumcise the males in his household (vv. 1-14).[64] Chapter 17 ends with the narrator's reports in vv. 23-27 that the patriarch followed divine orders.[65]

The heart of the pericope, vv. 15-21, returns to the matter of the appropriate heir for Abraham. It appears that there is a problem with the latest strategy of using a slave wife for establishing descent. No sooner is the birth of Ishmael recorded (though in chapter 17 he is now thirteen years old), the covenant of circumcision initiated, and the problem of an heir seemingly solved than we are told that Ishmael is not to be his father's lineal heir. He is not actually who the deity had in mind for Abraham's heir. Thus, we learn that Ishmael is not the son of the promise to Abram. Verse 16 reveals that the promise to Abram will be fulfilled by a child of Sarai's, now called Sarah. Chapter 17 incorporates the promise-fulfillment pattern in Genesis.[66] The child promised to Abram will be borne by Sarah.[67]

---

63. Genesis 17 is another version of the covenant established in chapter 15. Source analysis assigns these texts to different authors; the Yahwist and Elohist are responsible for Genesis 15 and the Priestly writer for Genesis 17. These two accounts also differ in their emphases: Genesis 17 focuses on progeny (only v. 8 mentions the promise of land) while Genesis 15 stresses both progeny and land.

64. A discussion of this text pointing out the lack of divine commitment can be found in D. N. Freedman, "Divine Commitment and Human Obligation: The Covenant Theme," *Int* 18 (1964) 425.

65. For information on the ritual of circumcision, see R. de Vaux, *Ancient Israel: Its Life and Institutions* (2 vols.; New York: McGraw-Hill, 1961) 1.46–48, 75–85.

66. Coats, *Genesis*, 136. Promise-fulfillment as a theme is a characteristic concern of the P source.

67. The position of the narrative sources, J, E, and P, on patrilineal descent in Genesis reveals that "a continuing tension between descent from fathers and descent from mothers is treated in three consistently different ways. P mostly refuses to acknowledge that such a problem exists. E, and especially J, recognize it, but J is willing to let it be, while E wants to correct it sacrificially; that is, the Yahwist alone tolerates 'bilateral' descent" (N. Jay, "Sacrifice, Descent and the Patriarchs," *VT* 38 [1988] 55). Jay's study does not analyze Genesis 17, since she

Consistent with cross-cultural data, the text now reveals the most acceptable option for maintaining the patrilineal descent line of Abraham. We learn it is not just that Abraham must be the father of the child; Sarah must be the mother. The strength and unity of the conjugal pair are affirmed as they were earlier when Sarai and Abram sojourned in Egypt (Gen 12:10—13:1).

So while Abram acts in good faith in fathering a child through a secondary wife, Hagar, the pattern of heirship extracted from the unfolding lives of Abraham, Sarah, and Hagar indicates that there is more to the correct solution to the problem of obtaining an heir than these individuals had previously realized. In order for Sarah and Abraham to become parents, Yahweh will reverse Sarah's barrenness.[68] Despite Abraham's laughter at the thought of Sarah bearing a child (v. 17)—foreshadowing and connecting with the laughter of the other parent to this child and heir (18:12)— God emphasizes that such a child will be born (v. 19). Of course, the name of the child, Isaac (that is, "he laughs"), will be wordplay on the laughter of his parents.[69]

In all of chapter 17, Abraham speaks only two verses (vv. 17-18), and these stem from his incredulity that Sarah could possibly bear a child and from his concern for Ishmael's future. It is as if Abraham challenges God and says, "Why can't you leave well enough alone? I have already fathered a child; why can't this son be my heir?" Suddenly Abraham, a man who for so many years was uncertain about his lineage, is confronted with the possibility that he will have two sons, and not insignificantly, they will be from different mothers. The situation will raise new perspectives on strategies of heirship and provide further information on how a man determines his lineal descendant in accordance with certain social structures.

Finally, Abraham pleads that God look favorably upon Ishmael (v. 18). In response God promises, "I will bless him and make him fruitful and multiply him exceedingly; he shall be the father of twelve princes, and I will make him a great nation" (v. 20). Ishmael

says, "P does not tell any of these great stories" (70). When her conclusions are joined with my own, it appears both E and P have a concern with the proper patrilineage for the Israelite descent line.

68. Thus, by implication, Yahweh becomes the source of the progeny all along.

69. See Gen 17:17; 18:12, 13, 15; 21:3, 6. On the name Isaac, see Westermann, *Genesis 12–36,* 269.

receives a promise from God, but with Abraham and his descendants the deity makes a covenant whose sign is circumcision.[70] The text is meaningful on two levels, individual and national. First, Isaac, not Ishmael, is Abraham's lineal descendant. Second, the descendants of Abraham and Isaac have rights to the land of Canaan (v. 8), but the descendants of Ishmael do not—even though they will be a great nation. In this analysis, literary judgments on the theme of promise and kinship perspectives on heirship explain the political function of descent lines and family structure in the Sarah-Hagar cycle.

Genesis 18:1-15

The plot of this narrative cycle moves next to the episode in 18:1-15, the visit of the three divine messengers to Abraham and Sarah with news of the future birth of an heir to the couple. Sarah's laughter in v. 12 harks back to the response of Abraham in 17:17 upon hearing this announcement. Both Sarah and Abraham are part of the plan for this heir; both must hear for themselves of Yahweh's intentions.[71] The marriage bond is affirmed, as it was in Gen 12:10—13:1 and 17:15-21. In fact, several times within the announcement of the impending birth of a son the text reminds us of the nature of their relationship: twice Yahweh says to Abraham, "Sarah your wife" (vv. 9, 10), and once Sarah refers to Abraham not by his proper name but as "my husband" (v. 12).

The story uses Sarah's changed name—rather than calling her Sarai—suggesting that this unit should be read together with the previous pericope; in chapter 17 God renames her. The two texts depend upon each other; the second advances the first—that is, the motif of the promised son is developed further. Whereas Genesis 17 includes the general news that Sarah will bear a child, Genesis 18 comments specifically about the event. Sarah will become a

---

70. On circumcision as a sign of membership in the lineage, see H. Eilberg-Schwartz, *The Savage in Judaism* (Bloomington and Indianapolis: Indiana Univ. Press, 1990) 167–76.

71. In 18:1-15, the action focuses on Sarah and her involvement with the messengers; Abraham is basically a shadowy figure in the interaction of the characters. The news that Sarah will bear a child comes directly to her (cf. Judges 13). Because Sarai's barrenness is the source of the disequilibrium that has plagued Abraham's line since 11:30, it is not surprising that she is depicted so fully here, now that she is about to get from her life what she has wanted so much.

mother in the spring (vv. 10, 14). Together the two episodes make clear how the plan to increase the descent line of Abraham is to be enacted: Yahweh plans to reverse Sarah's infertility,[72] despite the advanced ages of Sarah and Abraham (vv. 11-12). The situation is all the more miraculous because "it had ceased to be with Sarah according to the way of women" (v. 11). After Abraham tries several alternative strategies for heirship—those involving Lot, Eliezer, and Ishmael—the text finally specifies that only a child born of the union of Abraham and Sarah can legitimately be considered their heir. From a literary perspective, the promise to Abraham of a son finds fulfillment in Sarah's future child. From the point of view of comparative anthropology, the preferred strategy for heirship is a son borne by Sarah to Abraham. The mechanism for advancing the genealogy of Abraham is set in motion through Yahweh's stipulations.

Just as the present narrative of the life of Abraham foreshadows but contrasts with the following one on the life of Lot and how he obtains heirs (Genesis 19), both address the topic of the appropriate hospitality when receiving guests.[73] Both Abraham and Lot receive their heirs in conjunction with the travels of the messengers who visit them. However, the women who bear them these

---

72. If the barren wife (Sarah, Rebekah, Rachel, Hannah, Samson's mother; cf. the Shunammite woman in 2 Kings 4) were not a literary motif, instead of a proven biological fact, one might raise questions about the ancient Israelite's knowledge of procreation. Cross-cultural data suggest that in contexts with a patrilineal descent line, a couple's failure to produce a child is routinely blamed on the wife without any consideration of the possibility that the husband could be the cause of the problem. Thus, we are given a male interpretation of a biological problem; for example, J. Beale, *Women in Ireland* (Bloomington and Indianapolis: Indiana Univ. Press, 1987) 27–28. The texts present problems from the male perspective. Inasmuch as the matter of barrenness is always resolved in the stories, it is impossible to speak of the fate of a couple who do not eventually produce a biological heir.

73. R. C. Culley compares Gen 18:1-8 with 19:1-3 but is unable to account for the similarities between them (R. C. Culley, *Studies in the Structure of Hebrew Narrative* [Philadelphia: Fortress; Missoula, Mont.: Scholars Press, 1976] 54–55). Van Seters believes that the similarities are deliberate (van Seters, *Abraham in History*, 215–17). For discussions emphasizing the original independence of chapters 18 and 19, see Kilian, "Überlieferungsgeschichte Lots," 23–37; and Noth, *Pentateuchal Traditions*, 151–54. An analysis relating Genesis 19 to Judges 19, but arguing for the chronological priority of the latter, is found in S. Niditch, "The 'Sodomite' Theme in Judges 19-20: Family, Community, and Social Disintegration," *CBQ* 44 (1982) 365–78. See also S. Lasine, "Guest and Host in Judges 19: Lot's Hospitality in an Inverted World," *JSOT* 29 (1984) 37–59.

heirs are treated in contrasting manners upon the arrival of these messengers to their households. The contrasting fates of these women provide us with information about the place of women in the Israelite household as represented through the family stories in Genesis.

Genesis 18:16—19:38

Abraham's intercessory role for Sodom and Gomorrah in Gen 18:16-33 bears a resemblance to his earlier involvement in the wars of the kings of the East (Genesis 14). In both situations, kinship responsibilities determine Abraham's actions; in both episodes, the fate of his nephew Lot is threatened due to the tumultuous conditions in the land where he chose to live. Despite the geographical separation between Abraham and Lot, the kinship bond remains central to them. The stories suggest that Abraham and Lot are bound to help and protect each other insofar as each is aware of the dangerous circumstances the other one faces. As I mentioned earlier when analyzing chapter 14, kinship presupposes a political responsibility of one man for the other. Of course, Abraham's life is never threatened (despite his protests to the contrary in Genesis 20), while Lot appears always to be in danger once he leaves the protection of his uncle's household in chapter 13. Genesis 14 and 18:16—19:38 reflect the inextricable connection between political situations and kinship responsibilities. One understands Abraham's willingness to stand up and argue with Yahweh in the context of his responsibilities to Lot. Neither Abraham nor Yahweh ever explicitly mentions Lot in the dialogue in 18:16-33; nor is Lot ever known as a righteous man—despite Abraham's concern for the righteous. Yet with its emphasis on Sodom (18:16, 20, 22, 26), the story presupposes Lot, who was last reported to be near Sodom (Genesis 14) and who next appears "sitting in the gate of Sodom" (19:1).

Things initially go well for Lot when the messengers arrive. He offers them food and shelter and sees to their general comfort (19:1-3). Like Abraham in Genesis 18, Lot is a model host in chapter 19. Even Lot's willingness to offer his daughters to the men of Sodom and Gomorrah as sexual substitutes for the recently arrived messengers whom the local inhabitants desire reflects practices of honor and hospitality in the ancient Near East and has parallels in more recent studies.[74] The situation of Lot's daughters, who are offered as sexual partners for the local men, contrasts sharply with the situation of the decorous Sarah who, in 18:10, hides modestly behind the tent flap when these same messengers visit her home. The very possibility that Lot's daughters will become sexually involved with the men of Sodom and Gomorrah, due to the generosity of their father, foreshadows the ethnically impure (from the lineal Israelite perspective) genealogy that will be Lot's fate.[75]

Genesis 18:16—19:38 concludes the subplot of the fate of Lot, which began in 13:2-18 and continued in chapter 14. As noted earlier, these texts are all set around the site of Zoar.[76] Through the casual mention of the city in chapter 13, the reader is made aware of its existence, though not prepared for the function it will have in Lot's future. Zoar, the city where Lot flees from the destruction of Sodom and Gomorrah; Zoar, the small city, is the city of Lot's fate. It is the city toward which he has been journeying for his entire narrative existence. Yet, ironically, once Lot finally arrives at this small city he is too afraid to dwell in it and instead chooses to live in a cave. Even the small city is too big for Lot. The man who chose the big part of the land for himself in chapter 13 ends up in a small cave.[77] In consequence of this ultimate avoidance of the city of his fate, Lot dies to the Sarah-Hagar cycle after Genesis 19.

Another consequence of life in the cave outside Zoar is that

---

74. For example, J. A. Pitt-Rivers, "The Fate of Shechem or the Politics of Sex," *The Fate of Shechem or the Politics of Sex* (Cambridge Studies in Social Anthropology 19; Cambridge: Cambridge Univ. Press, 1977).

75. Lot's actions in offering his daughters to the men of Sodom and Gomorrah suggest that rules of honor take priority over those of morality. Social custom appears to demand no less. "It should be noted that when sanctuary is offered in the house or tent of an individual, the host gains honor through affording it, since it testifies to his power to protect" (Pitt-Rivers, *The Fate of Shechem*, 115). The similarities between the situation in 19:4-11 and Judg 19:22-25 are noted by Culley, *Structure of Narrative*, 56–59.

76. Consider the wordplay in 19:20, *miṣ'ār* (it is small). On the tradition-historical issues raised by the Lot traditions, see Noth, *Pentateuchal Traditions*, 151–54. Noth argues that the Lot traditions became associated with a cave outside Zoar, but that they did not originate there; he believes that it is presently impossible to trace their origin (153).

77. Helyer argues that as part of the message of chapters 18–19 a moralistic comparison is drawn between Abraham and Lot that leads to the conclusion "that human initiative—Lot's choice—always leads to catastrophe" (Helyer, "Separation of Abram and Lot," 84).

the sexual relationship that takes place there between Lot and his daughters establishes the genealogical line of Lot.[78] The story about Lot shares with the Abraham story the literary concern with a son(s) to continue their father's line.[79] Before the Sarah-Hagar cycle can be concluded, resolution comes to the descent lines of all the individuals introduced in the genealogy of Terah.

Circumstances of destruction in Sodom and Gomorrah leave Lot's daughters convinced that there are no men left to father their children, and, thus, they turn to their father for this purpose.[80] The heinous act of incest witnesses to the women's commitment to bear children: they will do whatever is necessary—go against all taboos—in order to have children.[81] Although their actions ultimately provide for the continuance of their father's line, the text never specifies that in having sexual intercourse with their father the daughters are concerned to perpetuate their father's lin-

78. Presumably Silberman's passing remarks on this episode are an oblique reminder of the drunken Noah and his sons, who should be compared with the drunken Lot and his daughters. He writes, "The long novella of Sodom and Gomorrah...[is] concluded by the dalliance of Lot's daughters with their drunken father, echoing a much earlier occurrence of that motif deeper in the well of the past" ("Listening to the Text," 21).

79. H. C. Brichto, "Kin, Cult, Land and Afterlife—A Biblical Complex," HUCA 44 (1973) 27.

80. Much scholarly ink has been spilled debating whether or not the cave story in vv. 30-38 is original to the traditions of Lot. The mention of Zoar and the question of bridegrooms for the daughters are presupposed in vv. 30-38; thus, all of chapter 19 should be read together; all parts of it depend upon each other for meaning. In support of the unity of Genesis 19, see A. Baumgarten, "A Note on the Book of Ruth," JANESCU 5 (1973) 11-12; von Rad, Genesis, 211-20; van Seters, Abraham in History, 219-20. For the opposite viewpoint, see R. Kilian, Die vorpriesterlichen Abrahams-Überlieferungen literarkritisch und traditionsgeschichtlich untersucht (BBB 24; Bonn: P. Hanstein, 1966) 141-44.

81. See Vawter, On Genesis, 242: "A man of timid faith, destined to be mastered by events rather than to master them, Lot now supinely sacrifices the dignity of his person to unholy and forbidden relationships (see Leviticus 18:6-18) accomplished on him by his voracious daughters whose dignity he had earlier disregarded (vs. 8 above). They reward his many shortcomings as a man and as a father with the incestuous conception." Of course, one does not know if such taboos may be presupposed when interpreting these texts. On the one hand, the union of father and daughter(s) for procreation is never listed as an option in social-scientific discussion on heirship. On the other hand, such discussions make very clear that ultimately one must do whatever is necessary in order to perpetuate the lineage. In a context of few men, a woman must choose from a limited pool of partners. Lot's daughters appear to recognize this. The kinship relationship—even if it is a segmented one—between the Israelites and the Ammonites and Moabites, appears to validate the daughters' decision; see chapter 4 n. 27, below.

eage. Their desire to obtain offspring through their father, while it accomplishes the former, appears, rather, to be motivated by concerns for their own social standing. Lot's drunkenness renders him passive, and presumably nearly unconscious, throughout the episode. His inactivity contrasts with his daughters' initiative in working to preserve a family.[82] Lot's lineage is perpetuated, even though Lot was in a drunken stupor when he created his own descendants.[83] His passivity here mirrors his passivity in Genesis 14.

The narrator never outrightly condemns what happened between the daughters and their father in the cave outside Zoar. The offspring of this union, the Moabites and the Ammonites (vv. 37-38), result in a non-Israelite descent line for Lot—even though on a national level the Moabites and Ammonites are part of the larger segmented kinship group of the ancient Near East. Mention of the Moabites and the Ammonites shifts the story's concern from the family level to the national level. The Moabites and Ammonites are part of the larger kinship group of the Israelites.

Based on a comparison with the Sarah and Abraham story, the narrative in chapter 19 provides information bearing on the Israelite perspective on the proper union for obtaining children. In the case of Sarah and Abraham, a monogamous marriage results in a lineal heir for the Israelite descent group begun by Terah. In the case of Lot, the union of the wrong sexual partners, the relationship of a father and his daughters, produces a non-Israelite genealogy. Based on kinship analysis, Lot's daughters' inappropriate strategy of heirship results in the Moabites and Ammonites being excluded from the lineal descendants of Terah, just as inappropriate heirship patterns will remove Ishmael and his descendants, the Ishmaelites, from this lineage (Gen 21:21b). Yet the Ammonites, Moabites, and Ishmaelites are part of the segmented genealogy of Terah, but not his lineal one. The subplot, the

---

82. As Westermann remarks, "These are indications that in all probability we must review the prevailing opinion that in the ancient history of Israel the man alone was the determining party. Gen 16; 19; 27 indicate that by way of exception and in cases of extreme necessity the woman could take the initiative. In any case women had a greater importance in patriarchal times than is generally acknowledged" (*Genesis 12–36*, 315).

83. Thus, in contrast to A. Lods, the story is much more than a tale of the origin of humanity. See A. Lods, "La caverne de Lot," *RHR* 95 (1927) 204–19.

life of Lot, offers a sociological contrast to the situation whereby Abraham obtains his heir.

With the case of the lineage of Lot, we have access to different levels of social analysis. Lot's family history allows for the development of both family and nation. Taken together the Abraham and Lot narratives explore the reproduction of the Israelite patrilineal descent group; this group has blood ties to the larger geographical community of the ancient Near East, and yet it presumably denigrates the non-Israelite kin.

Unlike the other narratives in Genesis that focus on two women—each trying to produce a child/children for the husband (that is, Sarah and Hagar, and Rachel and Leah),[84] and each story being marked by the intense rivalry that appears to characterize the lives of women in a variation of co-wife pairing—the story of Lot's two daughters illustrates a situation of two women supporting each other for the purpose of guaranteeing their future. Whether their concern is with the social status of motherhood or the protection mothers can expect from their sons is not clear. The minimal portrayal of the daughters suggests that the lack of rivalry between them is not common in daily life. That is, in the case of Sarah and Hagar, and then later Rachel and Leah, the women are fully developed as characters. They breathe narrative life, and we are given a glimpse of the situations that energize them at this stage in the cycle of family life. However, Lot's daughters are mere mirrors of each other; neither is developed as an individual in her own right. The two say exactly the same words.[85] Their mutual interchangeability is underscored by the fact that their names are never given. They are ciphers. Yet in order that each daughter have a child, their social personality is expressed. Anthropological analysis of these literary judgments leads us to the conclusion that the omission of Lot's daughters' names may be a comment on the infrequent situation of women working together—because in a patrilineal society their interests rarely coincide. In such a con-

---

84. See 1 Samuel 1 regarding Hannah and Penninah.

85. Despite the importance of this text, Otwell understands it simply as an illustration of a situation where the mother names her child. But even in this regard, the two sisters mirror each other: each names her child with an etiological sentence (Otwell, *And Sarah Laughed,* 112). Further study is needed to determine whether Lot's daughters are unique in being mirrors of each other or whether there are other examples of this characterization in Hebrew Bible narrative.

text, women are typically forced to compete against each other for a place within their husband's household and lineage. Here we may think back to the jealousy and strife between Sarah and Hagar in Genesis 16. However, later we will see that while Rachel and Leah initially had reason to compete against each other for Jacob's favor, ultimately the sisters unite because of their common interest in leaving Laban's household.

Genesis 19:31 suggests that Lot's daughters are the final commentators on the life of their father. When the daughters refer to their father as *zāqēn* (an old man), they may have categories of sexuality in mind. The use of this same root occurred in 18:11-13, where it refers to the old age of Sarah and Abraham as this affects their ability to have children.[86] The use of *zāqēn* in the Lot story suggests that Lot's manner of establishing a lineage should be compared with Abraham's attempt to do likewise.

The importance of *zāqēn* connects with the following words in the verse: *wě'îš 'ên* (a man there is not). Hebrew syntax is reversed: typically, the negative *'ên* occurs in the construct before the noun.[87] Word order reversal in v. 31b may be a means used by the narrator to emphasize Lot's advanced age in 31a. Lot is so old that he cannot do what men typically do, that is, take care of their families. Lot's advanced age may play a part in Lot's passivity when his sons/grandsons are conceived; he is not even aware of his sexual role when he fathers children through his daughters. Twice

---

86. The issue of sexuality is also brought up in a subtle way earlier, in 19:14, when Lot's sons-in-law think him to be "joking" (*kimṣaḥēq*) when he instructs them to flee for their lives. As will be argued below in connection with 21:9, the piel of *ṣḥq* (to laugh) has strong sexual connotations each time it occurs; I believe it can only be interpreted sexually. In 19:14, a piel participle of this root is used. Could the sons-in-law intend a double entendre and be referring both to the sexual interaction that the men of Sodom and Gomorrah want with the three messengers and the sexual activities with his daughters that Lot tries to arrange in lieu of these messengers? If so, 19:14 might be translated, "But his sons-in-law thought he was referring to the sexual threat posed by the local inhabitants." Possibly the sons-in-law are speaking with tongue-in-cheek and commenting on Lot here just as later the daughters in the cave may be speaking with tongue-in-cheek of their father as an old man and yet the only source of sons available to them. As to how the daughters can be virgins in v. 8, then both engaged and married to these sons-in-law in vv. 12 and 14, see Kilian, *Abrahams-Überlieferungen*, 115–16. The marital status of the daughters presumed in these texts is ultimately of little importance; what matters, in light of the events in the cave in vv. 30-38, is that earlier men had been available who could have fathered offspring with the daughters, but now these men are presumed dead.

87. *GKC* 480.

Lot's daughters get Lot drunk, and each time he unknowingly has sexual intercourse with one of them. Verse 31 suggests that Lot has never acted according to the role expectations of Israelite men, which stands in contrast to Abraham's seemingly exemplary behavior.

Genesis 20:1-18

The concern in 20:1-18 shifts from Lot back to Abraham. It begins with information about a journey, though it provides no specific rationale for Abraham and Sarah dwelling in Gerar. We are simply told, "From there Abraham journeyed to the territory of the Negeb, and settled between Kadesh and Shur. He sojourned in Gerar" (v. 1). Like Gen 12:10—13:1 before it, the narrative recounts another attempt by Abraham to be rid of his barren wife, Sarah; Abraham again exploits a visit to a foreign land as an opportunity to represent his wife as his sister in order to remove her from his household.[88] This is the fourth (Gen 12:10—13:1; 15:1-21; 16:1-15; 20:1-18) and final situation that demonstrates that, without a child to validate her position in the household, Sarah is expendable to Abraham; he will find a solution to the problem of an heir without her. The announcement that Sarah will bear a child in the following year does not seem to affect Abraham in his determination to be rid of his wife.

This circumstance of infertility appears to make Sarah vulnerable to Abraham's words and actions. After arriving in Gerar in v. 1, Abraham—without provocation—blurts out about Sarah: "She is my sister" (v. 2). Only Yahweh's intervention (vv. 3-7) brings Abraham's scheme to an end and restores the conjugal unit to its original state. Most of the chapter is devoted to resolving the wife-sister ruse: Yahweh explains the situation, Abimelech protests his innocence, and Abraham insists, "I did it because I thought, There is no fear of God at all in this place, and they will kill me because of my wife" (v. 11). Moreover, Abraham tells Abimelech that while Sarah is in fact his wife, she truly is his sister, that is, his kinswoman; they are from the same patrilineage (v. 12).[89] The

---

88. While source critics attribute Gen 12:10—13:1 to the Yahwist, Genesis 20 is said to come from the Elohist.

89. On the likelihood that they are kin, see chapter 1, above. D. Steinmetz notes

money given to Abraham by Abimelech as vindication for Sarah (20:15) may possibly be interpreted as the narrator's confirmation that Sarah was innocent of any designs of her own to separate husband and wife, and suggests the veracity of Abraham's statement. The Bible gives no further information on the relationship between Sarah and Abraham. That the two belong together would seem to be stressed by the phrase "Abraham's wife" in 20:18. The threat to the husband-wife relationship of Abraham and Sarah explains why Yahweh had closed the wombs of the women in Abimelech's house. Sarah's present infertility connects with the infertility of the women of Gerar.

Other than in the dream sequence, the narrative depicts incidents in which only the men of the story speak, though a woman is the cause of their dialogue. Sarah is never heard from directly; Abraham speaks about her and Abimelech to her. Sarah's response is never recorded. It is interesting that when Abraham defends the truth of his earlier assertion that his wife is his sister (20:12), he notes that he had previously given her instructions on what to say when they were out traveling together.[90] The husband informs his wife of the words she is to use when someone speaks to her. Specifically, Abraham has told Sarah to tell others that she is his sister. From v. 5 we learn that Sarah did exactly what she was told; she tells Abimelech precisely what Abraham instructed her to say. The narrative suggests that the wife is bound—especially the barren wife—to do as her husband says. This assessment is confirmed by cross-cultural studies of women in patrilineal societies. Such studies explain that a woman's status within the household depends upon her reproductive role, and that until she fulfills this role she is basically an outsider to her husband's family.[91]

Genesis 21:1-21

The resolution of the plot of the Sarah-Hagar cycle comes in 21:1-21. Sarah's barrenness is overcome through Yahweh's intervention; Isaac is born (vv. 1-2). No sooner does Sarah become a

---

that even though Abraham and Sarah may be kin, they are still married to each other; see D. Steinmetz, *From Father to Son* (Louisville: Westminster/John Knox Press, 1991) 65.

90. See Pitt-Rivers, *The Fate of Shechem*, 159.

91. Michaelson and Goldschmidt, "Female Roles," 330–49, esp. 348.

mother than a complication arises: now she wants Hagar and Ishmael banished from the household. Social-scientific studies help
us understand the course of events. Abraham does as his wife demands due to her status as primary wife and mother.[92] Explicit in
Sarah's desires and actions is the question: Which of Abraham's
two sons will be his heir? Sarah works to secure a firm and future position for herself in Abraham's household through the birth
of her son. Sarah's actions have cross-cultural analogues that reveal how a woman's power comes through her son. A son is his
mother's source of status and the focus of her attention when he
is young. As a result of this maternal devotion, as a youth a boy
becomes emotionally bound to his mother (see Gen 24:26b). When
the son grows up, he provides his mother with protection—both
physically and politically. In other words, a woman's affective ties
are to her son, not her husband.[93] Anthropological analysis yields
the following sense of events in the life cycle of a woman in ancient Israel: "Being a woman is not enough, one has to become a
wife. Being a wife is not enough, one has to become a mother."[94] I
would add to this: Being a mother is not enough, one must be the
mother of her husband's heir.

Hence, Sarah is concerned that Ishmael and his mother leave
their home with her and Abraham in order that Isaac alone will
inherit from his father. Then, she will be guaranteed Isaac's devotion and protection; he will be indebted to her for her efforts in
making him Abraham's lineal heir. Through kinship studies the
legal situation becomes clear: the son borne by the primary wife
is automatically entitled as his father's heir. The son who will not
inherit from his father is expected to leave home, something that
Ishmael has not done. This factor, coupled with rivalry, motivates

---

92. Westermann notes that in both 16 and 21 a quarrel between women leads
to Abraham playing the role of intermediary. What he does not discuss is that
both episodes present a situation where the wife gets her way; Abraham must
do as his wife demands (Westermann, *Promises*, 63–64). On a woman's status as
mother, see Michaelson and Goldschmidt, "Female Roles," 338.

93. Collier, "Women in Politics," 92; Michaelson and Goldschmidt, "Female
Roles." On the plight of a woman without a male to protect her, see P. S. Hiebert,
" 'Whence Shall Help Come to Me?' The Biblical Widow," *Gender and Difference
in Ancient Israel* (ed. P. L. Day: Minneapolis: Fortress, 1989) 125–41. Westbrook
notes that a widow might be denied her dowry by her husband's heir (*Property
and the Family*, 154–55).

94. K. R. Andriolo, "Myth and History: A General Model and Its Application
to the Bible," *American Anthropologist* 83 (1981) 272.

Sarah to expel Hagar. Despite the status differential that separates Sarah from her handmaid, she appears to want no reminder of the years when Hagar looked down upon her.

Implications of Genesis 16 and 21

We are now ready to analyze the implications of events in Genesis 16 and 21. When a primary wife is unable to bear a child for her husband, a concubine, a secondary wife, may be a legitimate option for obtaining progeny. Together, these two chapters reflect not only the legal ramifications of inheritance decisions on family structure but also the effect of such decisions on individual behavior. In polycoity, conflict normally occurs between the co-wives, and this remains true even when the women are of equal legal status. The situation in the Sarah-Hagar cycle concerns women of different statuses. In the case of Sarah and Hagar, on a legal level, the wife is superior to the concubine, but the pregnancy of the maidservant leads to jealousy and rivalry between them. Legal and psychological factors intermingle when both women become mothers; because the status of the child is linked to the status of its mother, and only one son can function as Abraham's heir, Sarah demands that Hagar and Ishmael be banished. The course of action is determined by the legality of Isaac's claim to be his father's lineal heir, because a primary marriage—such as Sarah and Abraham have—is established for property concerns while concubinage separates property from procreation.

Now we must ask a further question about the events of chapter 21. Ishmael's behavior at a party for Isaac (vv. 8-9) convinces Sarah of the urgency of banishing Hagar and Ishmael from the household, in order to secure her position and that of her son. We have already interpreted the significance of Sarah's request. What is not clear is exactly what Ishmael was doing in Gen 21:9 that Sarah saw and made her think of matters of inheritance.[95] Presumably it was something she had never seen Ishmael doing

---

95. Silberman offers the following interpretation of these events: "Its real meaning, hidden under a series of wordplays, may be that Sarah sees that the son of her rival, Hagar, has been and may continue to be *mṣḥq*, the joy of his father to the exclusion of her son *yṣḥq* who is for her the joy-giver" ("Listening to the Text," 21).

before; otherwise how are we to explain that only at this moment
do questions of inheritance occur to Sarah?

There is a long history of difficulty in making sense of this
passage. The translators of the Septuagint added "with her son
Isaac" after the end of the verse. Thus, Ishmael and Isaac are seen
as playing together. However, one must consider the possibility
that the phrase about Isaac was added in the LXX to render less
objectionable a text with original explicit sexual meaning. The fact
that the root used here, ṣḥq, has sexual connotations in the piel—
the same verbal stem used in v. 9—suggests an argument for the
sexual nature of Ishmael's actions (without Isaac).[96] Ishmael's actions prompt Sarah to remember that in order to insure Isaac's
place as next of kin to Abraham, Ishmael must be removed from
the household. Ishmael's sexual actions have direct bearing on the
genealogical concerns of the family stories in Genesis.

Having changed statuses—moving from barren primary wife
to mother of her husband's heir—Sarah achieves her goal in Abraham's family. Now that an heir has been found for Abraham's
patrilineal descent line, the cycle of Sarah's life, and the conjugal
unit of Sarah and Abraham, as the focus of the narrative cycle,
rapidly draws to an end. Abraham has designated an heir in accordance with the social structure, and Sarah has made clear that
she has a legitimate role in the family unit. But not only does Sarah
secure her future in Abraham's family by providing him with an
heir; having removed Ishmael, Sarah has also worked to secure
her future under Isaac's care in the event that she should outlive
her husband. Significantly, Sarah's last words insist upon the ban-

---

96. The root ṣḥq occurs in the piel in Gen 19:14 (Lot's sons-in-law; see n. 86
above); 21:9; 26:8 (Isaac and Rebekah in Gerar); 39:14, 17 (Joseph and Potiphar's
wife); Exod 32:6 (Golden Calf); and Judg 16:25 (Samson and the Philistines).
All these texts can be interpreted to have strong sexual connotations. I believe
that in 21:9 the evidence suggests that Ishmael was alone and doing something
sexual that reminded Sarah of the topic of offspring and the continuance of
genealogy; Ishmael was masturbating. (Does the narrator intend a pun here on
the laughter of Abraham and Sarah and the name of their child—all from the root
ṣḥq?) The range of ṣḥq in the piel would appear to include masturbation (Gen
21:9), heterosexual activity (Gen 26:8), and homosexual involvement (Judg 16:25).
For a more traditional reading of 21:9, emphasizing that the two boys playing
together would stir up maternal jealousy in Sarah and prompt her to take action
against Ishmael, see von Rad, *Genesis*, 232. Hackett ("Rehabilitating Hagar," 20–
21) understands Ishmael's actions as "playing like Isaac"—that is, acting like an
heir to Abraham. Hence, she too interprets Sarah's motives at this point to relate
to a maternal concern that Isaac be Abraham's sole heir.

ishment of Ishmael and his mother in order that Isaac alone will inherit from Abraham. Yahweh's assent to this plan affirms that an heir for Abraham has been found at last.[97]

Genesis 21 resolves the problem of childlessness that Sarah faced since she was first introduced in 11:29-30. Further, it establishes the fate of Hagar and Ishmael as wilderness people (vv. 14-21). The remaining episodes of the Sarah-Hagar cycle deal with issues of heirship and inheritance between Abraham and his son Isaac. Genesis 21:22—25:11 advances the plot forward so that we are prepared for stories about heirship in the generation of Isaac. The Sarah-Hagar cycle comes to an end with narrative units that confirm Isaac as heir and tie together the details of Abraham's life.

Heirship and Inheritance

Genesis 21:22-34

In Genesis 21:22-34, Abraham negotiates with Abimelech (who is the king of Gerar in 20:2) and Phicol, his commander. Abraham complains that Abimelech's servants stole a well (v. 25) that Abraham dug (v. 30). After Abimelech protests his innocence—that is, he says he knows nothing about the situation (cf. Gen 20:5)—the two men make a covenant that assures Abraham's water rights (vv. 27-32). This brief text focuses on matters of property, which are a primary concern for the inheritance Isaac will eventually receive from his father, Abraham.

Genesis 22:1-19

When Yahweh tests Abraham to determine whether or not he will sacrifice his son, we appear to have the deity's affirmation of the strength of heirship that has come to Abraham's family line

---

97. Given the narrative focus on Sarah's headstrong determination to banish Ishmael in order to secure her son's and her own position in Abraham's household, I question von Rad's conclusion that it was only *by coincidence* that Sarah's plan and Yahweh's plan for the future of this family converged here (*Genesis*, 232–33).

through the birth of Isaac.[98] The story's suspense is built up by the recurrence of the motif of "the beloved son."[99] Repetition of kinship terms, "father" and "son," reminds us of the trials and tribulation that Abraham experienced before Isaac was born, and of all that he as a father will lose if his son Isaac dies.

Not without interest is the fact that for the first time since the stories of Abram and Sarai began in 11:27 the narrative bears witness to the emotion of love: Abraham loves Isaac.[100] If we compare Gen 22:2 with Gen 21:10, the contrast is striking. In 21:10, Sarah is concerned about the rivalry between herself and her son, on the one hand, and Hagar and her son, on the other hand—for reasons related to inheritance. Her words and actions reflect a concern with status and not with emotion. In Gen 22:2, the mention of Isaac as Abraham's only son may also refer to status because at this point in the Sarah-Hagar cycle, Isaac is Abraham's lineal heir.

Genesis 22:20-24

Mention of Rebekah in 22:23 provides narrative preparation for Abraham's death.[101] News of her birth to Bethuel, son of Nahor, represents a shift in the pattern of presentation of genealogical information. As in 11:27-32, so in 22:20-24, information on the presence of women in the family interrupts the typical flow of information on men. Rebekah is the only person named—either man or woman—from the second generation of descendants from Nahor. Her name in the center of this genealogy anticipates the topic of a bride for Isaac; before Isaac can move into the position of lineal heir to his father and begin the cycle of his adult life, he must be established in his own family unit; he can become "a man" only once he has a genealogically appropriate wife.[102]

---

98. Helyer ("Separation of Abram and Lot," 84) comments that this is the seventh but greatest crisis in the narrative cycle of Abraham's life.

99. References to Isaac as Abraham's son are found in both direct address and third-person narrative description. See vv. 2, 3, 6, 7, 8, 9, 10, 12, 13, 16.

100. Although Abraham is concerned about the expulsion of Ishmael, the text never explicitly says that the reason for this concern is love for his son.

101. Silberman ("Listening to the Text," 22) considers the genealogy in 22:20-24 to be the beginning of the next narrative cycle.

102. See M. Z. Rosaldo ("The Use and Abuse of Anthropology: Reflections on Feminism and Cross-Cultural Understanding," *Signs* 5 [1980] 413) on marriage as a prerequisite for moving from boyhood to manhood.

Genesis 23:1-20

Only with the news that a woman from the correct descent line exists—news, to be sure, the reader is aware of but whose consequence is unknown to Isaac—does the text specifically mention Sarah's death. Sarah had been lost to the story since the birth of Isaac; now the details of her death and burial are made explicit. It is no coincidence that Sarah dies when Isaac has a new wife to replace his old mother.

In a pattern that we will see repeated again later with Rachel (Genesis 35), the barren wife Sarah dies her narrative death after having produced an heir. Once her fate is resolved, and once Isaac's future is secure, news of her death and burial are provided. The family stories in Genesis record the burial locations of the barren women only. Sarah and Rachel both suffer repeatedly from their barrenness; Genesis notes their final resting spots.[103] Sarah is buried in the cave of the Machpelah (23:19), while Rachel's tomb lies south of Jerusalem, near Bethlehem (35:19).[104] By contrast, the story never explicitly discusses the burials of the fertile matriarchs, Rebekah and Leah, though the deaths and burial spots of Abraham, Isaac, and Jacob are each recorded at the end of their narrative lives: Abraham (25:9-10), Isaac (35:27-29), Jacob (50:13). However, the narrative provides nothing more than an after-the-fact note of the deaths of Rebekah and Leah. This information is found in Gen 49:31 when Jacob tells Joseph that the two are buried in the same spot as the rest of the women and men whose lives are the focus of the Genesis family stories—that is, Abraham, Sarah, Isaac, Rebekah, and Leah all lie buried in the cave of Machpelah. The Sarah-Hagar cycle moves toward its conclusion with the death of one of the two members of the conjugal unit. The author is, however, less concerned with the impact of the news of Sarah's death on the family unit and more interested in describing how Abraham worked to secure land for a burial plot.[105] The text does briefly mention that Abraham mourned and wept for

---

103. On the grave traditions of these two, see Noth, *Pentateuchal Traditions*, 110, 113–14, 195 (Sarah); 85–86, 100 (Rachel).

104. According to 1 Sam 10:2 and Jer 31:15, Rachel's burial spot is north of Jerusalem.

105. On these negotiations, see Westbrook, *Property and the Family*, 24–35. Westbrook argues that Abraham "wishes to acquire an inheritable estate ('*hzh*), which can only be achieved by paying its full value" (106). Westermann (*Genesis 12–36,*

Sarah upon her death (v. 2), but then moves quickly to recount the diplomatic legal transactions that occurred between Abraham and the Hittite Ephron when the latter sold the former a burial place. Abraham's sense of loss upon his wife's death prepares the reader for Isaac's reaction to his mother's death in Gen 24:67.

Genesis 24:1-67

The pericope in Gen 24:1-67 is essential to the completion of the Sarah-Hagar cycle. The story provides extensive details on how, at his master's request, Abraham's servant secures a wife for Isaac. We are made keenly aware of the "kinship credentials" of the woman deemed appropriate (Rebekah is the daughter of Bethuel, who is a son of Nahor, who is a son of Terah—that is, Rebekah is a descendant of the Israelite patrilineage) for the son deemed appropriate heir to his father.[106] For not any woman will be a suitable wife for Isaac. Not only will the young bride be a mate for Isaac so that the patrilineal descent line can continue; she will also be the one responsible for filling the void in Isaac's life left by the death of his mother (24:67). That the negotiations surrounding the marriage of Isaac and Rebekah are conducted by Laban, Rebekah's brother, rather than by Bethuel, her father, may suggest that Bethuel had other wives. Possibly in this polygynous context, Bethuel was residing with another woman and so Laban acts as the family representative in the absence of his father.

From the list of gifts from Abraham that his servant delivers to Rebekah and her family, we may surmise that Abraham is a wealthy man. His son Isaac stands to inherit a considerable amount of property as his father's lineal heir. Moreover, Rebekah receives many goods when she marries (vv. 10, 22, 30, 35, 47, 53), emphasizing the economic basis of a union between a husband and his primary wife. Rebekah's indirect dowry enhances the marriage fund and secures her position in the household and that of any children she may bear in the future.

---

376) connects this passage, with its emphasis on family and a place to bury one's dead, with the exilic period.

106. I assume that the reason Abraham prohibits Isaac from returning to Haran is that the patrilineal inheritance of land demands that the heir live in Canaan. Genesis 12:7 states that Abraham's descendants will inherit Canaan. As discussed earlier, the reason Lot can no longer be Abraham's adopted heir is because he moves outside of Canaan in chapter 13.

The story reminds us of the complexities of a young woman moving into a strange household and competing against her mother-in-law (whether dead or alive) for the affections of the groom. Isaac loves Rebekah, and she fills the void in his life created by the death of the first woman he loved, his mother, Sarah (24:67). Thus, a new conjugal unit is created; this information rapidly advances the plot of the narrative cycle to a point where there is little left to tell about Abraham's generation—other than of his death.

Genesis 25:1-11

Genesis 25:1-11 concludes the Sarah-Hagar cycle. Abraham takes another wife, Keturah, before dying. This marriage can be understood as a union inferior to the one Abraham made with Sarah. As we learn, the marriage of Abraham and Keturah separates procreation from property. Even though the names of the sons born to him through her are listed, the narrator carefully emphasizes that these sons left Canaan and lived far away from Isaac.[107] On the basis of kinship studies we understand that the matter of inheritance, which was so carefully worked out with the birth of Isaac, must not be tampered with. Only he can be considered the heir to Abraham. So Abraham gave his inheritance to Isaac but recognized his paternal responsibility to these other children and gave them gifts (v. 6).[108]

Placed as it is after the report of Sarah's death and immediately prior to news of Abraham's passing, 25:1-6 suggests that Abraham married Keturah after Sarah died. Were that the case, the marriage would be categorized as serial monogamy. However, the story does not require Sarah's death. The inheritance arrangement by which Abraham provides for all his children indicates that she did not bring property to the marriage. Keturah can be categorized as a concubine wife.[109]

Narrative closure comes to Abraham's life and to the Sarah-Hagar cycle with the news of the patriarch's death and his burial

---

107. Silberman suggests that given all the trouble Abraham had in starting his first family, information on his second family may touch on the "laughing motif" in this narrative cycle (Silberman, "Listening to the Text," 22).

108. For further analysis of this narrative unit, see the discussion in chapter 1.

109. Westermann (*Genesis 12–36*, 396) argues that ambiguity surrounds the status of Keturah.

by his two sons, Ishmael and Isaac (vv. 7-10). The reintroduction
of Ishmael, after he was expelled from Abraham's household in
Genesis 21, serves the literary function of preparing us for the
genealogies of both of Abraham's sons as the beginning of the
next narrative cycle.

The story of the events of the life of Abraham is framed by
genealogical units noting his relationship to his wife Sarah. The
narratives of Abraham and Sarah began with the information in
11:27-32 that Sarah was his wife but that she was barren, and
end in 25:1-11 where we learn that upon his death Abraham was
buried next to his wife Sarah and that their son Isaac lived on
after them.

Chapter 3

The Rebekah Cycle: Monogamy

While the marriage arrangement of polycoity found in Gen 11:10—25:11 allows us to understand the family dynamics that develop when Abraham takes a secondary wife, Hagar, monogamy is the type of sexual union about which we are given information in Gen 25:12—35:29. Early in this narrative cycle, Rebekah's barrenness is overcome through Isaac's prayers to Yahweh (25:21). Rebekah bears Isaac two sons, Jacob and Esau, a situation that provides the reader with information about the resolution of descent and inheritance issues when a monogamous marriage yields more than one potential lineal heir. Both Esau and Jacob are legitimate heirs to their father's Israelite line; both have the same parents, which allows them to take their place in this lineage. I turn now to consider what issues determine which of Rebekah's two sons, Jacob or Esau, will inherit from their father, Isaac. My analysis will answer the question: Why are decisions of heirship in the generation of Isaac resolved in favor of Jacob and not Esau?

Genesis 25:12-18

The narratives that moved the genealogical cycle of Abraham's generation from beginning to end and clarified descent issues raised in the context of the genealogy of 11:27-32 now progress to a point that is structurally similar to the genealogical heading recording the generations of Shem. The genealogical superscription to the Rebekah cycle lists the ancestors of Ishmael, the son of Abraham who will not carry on the vertical Israelite lineage of his father. The genealogy of Ishmael in 25:12-18, like the genealogy of Shem, serves as the introduction to the genealogy of Isaac, the son whose descendants will transmit the Israelite line. Like the genealogy of Shem, the genealogy of Ishmael contains no narrative components. Instead, the stable progression of the family line from one generation to the next is recorded. Uninterrupted family stability, genealogical continuity, characterizes the history of Ishmael's descendants. In every respect, the record of the generations of Ishmael in Gen 25:12-18 is the structural equivalent to the generations of Shem in Gen 11:10-26.

Genesis 25:19-26

The genealogy of the son not chosen to carry on the Israelite heritage of his father moves forward to the genealogical unit concerning the chosen heir. In 25:19-26 the genealogy of the generation of Isaac's descendants begins. In structure, it follows the pattern last seen in the genealogy of Terah. The genealogy of Isaac introduces the stories of the descendants of Isaac, the events of whose lives will take the genealogy of their father forward to the next narrative cycle. In the case of Isaac, the narratives that follow his genealogy and give meaning to it concern the fate of his sons Jacob and Esau, born to him in his monogamous marriage to Rebekah. The genealogy of Isaac, like that of Terah earlier, introduces the stories of his children.

As would be expected from the precedent of the circumstances in the genealogy of Terah, the genealogy of Isaac introduces a situation of uncertainty in this man's family, which is potentially threatening to the continuance of his lineage. The stable family situation in the generations of Ishmael, one of Abraham's two sons, whose mother is his secondary wife, Hagar, stands in contrast with the complication in the generation of Isaac. Although we learn in 25:21 that Rebekah is barren—and because of Sarah's situation earlier we might believe that her condition will serve as the source of disruption in Isaac's family—Yahweh quickly corrects this family's affairs, and Rebekah becomes the mother of twin sons. But this seemingly harmonious situation actually creates a new problem of family heirship. If a man, Isaac, has two sons—borne moments apart by the same woman, Rebekah,[1] in a monogamous marriage arrangement—how is he to decide which one will be the lineal heir when Israelite custom has it that a man's descent line may pass through only one of his offspring?[2]

The rivalry set up between Jacob and Esau in 25:19-26 further complicates questions of inheritance from father to son in Isaac's generation.[3] In v. 23, Yahweh informs Rebekah of this rivalry with the information that the two will be divided against each other, and that one will be stronger than the other. The construction of the poetic piece leads the reader to believe that the stronger one is actually the older twin—the one whom Yahweh informs Rebekah will be a servant to the younger, weaker twin.[4] The poem suggests that, if indeed there was a customary priority given to the firstborn, as many assume, this right will be overturned in the case of

---

1. At this point in the narrative, no rule of primogeniture has been explicitly established. The story of the birthright in 25:29-34 does not clearly establish what possession of this right guarantees for Jacob, though it does foreshadow the fact that Esau is no longer a likely contender for the role of his father's lineal heir. Therefore, I find it difficult to agree with Westbrook, who argues that what is at stake here is the firstborn's right to a double share of the inheritance. Later, in Gen 27:29, according to Westbrook, Isaac also makes Jacob the administrator of the inheritance—that is, he gives him the right to determine when the inheritance will be divided so that he can obtain this double share (R. Westbrook, *Property and the Family in Biblical Law* [JSOTSup 113; Sheffield: JSOT Press, 1991] 137-38).

2. The narrative cycle connected with Isaac's genealogy raises important issues on the topic of heirship. In this regard, Speiser's remark that "Isaac, who can scarcely be described as a memorable personality in his own right, is important chiefly as a link in the patriarchal chain" fails to grasp the importance of the family history conveyed in the next body of texts (E. A. Speiser, *Genesis* [AB; Garden City, N.J.: Doubleday, 1964] 182). As L. H. Silberman comments, "In plot personality is of no great significance" ("Listening to the Text," *JBL* 102 [1983] 22).

3. For an analysis of the contrasting foci in the Sarah-Hagar and Rebekah cycles, see C. Westermann, *The Promises to the Fathers* (Philadelphia: Fortress, 1980) 74-76. While Westermann is correct that the former (which he labels the Abraham cycle) is concerned with issues of vertical genealogy and the latter (which he calls the Jacob/Esau cycle) with issues of horizontal genealogy (that is, the relationship between brothers), it is important to realize that the latter also ultimately stresses the vertical genealogical sequence. The Rebekah cycle directly addresses the question of who will be Isaac's lineal heir.

4. I follow commentators and assume poetic parallelism in interpreting which of the two sons will be stronger than the other.

Jacob and Esau. The rivalry between the two sons is evident from the moment they are born; although Esau is ready to be born first, Jacob grabs onto his heel in the womb and seemingly supplants Esau as the firstborn son (vv. 25-26).

This genealogical story challenges family harmony and serves as the introduction to the narratives that will advance family relationships from being dysfunctional back to another pristine state of genealogical progress. What follows then are the details of the cycle of events in the generation of Isaac's sons. Only through the connection between the genealogy in 25:19-26 and the narratives in 25:27—35:29 does meaning flow to either. The resolution of family conflict in the narratives of the Rebekah cycle advances the genealogical plot to a stage at which an uninterrupted genealogical progression from father to lineal heir is once again established.

Genesis 25:27-34

Genesis 25:27-34 presents the first occurrence, outside of the genealogy described above, of the central problem disturbing the generation of Isaac and Rebekah's offspring: the fierce rivalry between Jacob and Esau.[5] The significance of this literary motif can be interpreted in light of kinship studies. As literary-critical analysis illustrates, this competition between brothers is exemplified through the contrasting occupations of Jacob and Esau; the former is a shepherd while the latter is a hunter, signifying different life-styles. Further, one parent loves one son while the other parent favors the other son. Finally, privileges associated with being the firstborn son are emphasized when Esau sells his birthright to Jacob in a moment of weakness occasioned by hunger.[6] As a result of this transaction, Esau feels bitter (v. 34). The priority Jacob gains, privileges that theoretically belong to Esau, coincides with

---

5. The significance of this rivalry for the question of Isaac's heir is analyzed from the perspective of structural anthropology in K. R. Andriolo, "A Structural Analysis of Genealogy and Worldview in the Old Testament," *American Anthropologist* 75 (1973) 1657–69. None of Andriolo's conclusions stand in conflict with the ones reached in this study.

6. See M. Fishbane ("Composition and Structure in the Jacob Cycle [Gen 25:19—35:22]," *JJS* 26 [1975] 21–23) for discussion of Gen 25:19-34 and the importance of the birthright theme in it.

the rivalry already existent between them. Thus, the plot of the genealogy of Isaac deepens; the story clearly communicates the tension that characterizes this family with its twin sons who themselves complicate questions of inheritance when the elder sells his natural birthright to the younger. As the text implies, and as events in the Rebekah cycle will eventually demonstrate, social custom in ancient Israel demands that the chosen heir to the father's vertical lineage possess this birthright.[7]

The curious favoritism of each parent for a different son significantly affects further developments in the plot of the Rebekah cycle. These contrasting feelings can be interpreted from the perspective of comparative kinship studies. The tension that divides the family against itself is predicated on the split between Isaac and Esau, on the one hand, and Rebekah and Jacob, on the other hand.[8] By interrelating 25:27-34 with the preceding unit, Gen 25:19-26, one presumes that Rebekah's favoritism results from the information she received at the time of the birth of Jacob and Esau (25:23). By contrast, Isaac's feelings appear to derive from the fact that Esau was to be his firstborn, according to v. 25; hence, to him belongs the family birthright. In accordance with social custom, then, Esau is expected to receive special advantage from his father, Isaac, and to be his favorite.

However, in accordance with principles already operating in the story of Sarah's attempt to secure her son Isaac's position in the household—in order to legitimate her own place and guarantee her future security through the loyalty of her son in return for her efforts on his behalf—Rebekah takes the side of Jacob (v. 28).[9] Again, she presumably does this on the basis of the knowledge imparted to her by Yahweh in the earlier oracle. Although Isaac is unaware of it, Rebekah already knows that Jacob will dominate his brother Esau. Thus, she intends to secure the loyalty of Jacob in order that he will use his future power to her benefit. The Rebekah cycle begins with the picture of a family divided

---

7. For an attempt to make sense of the legal implications of possession of the birthright in light of Hurrian social customs, see Speiser, Genesis, 196–97, 212–13.

8. For further analysis of these same issues with special attention to literary style, see R. Alter, The Art of Biblical Narrative (New York: Basic Books, 1981) 42–45.

9. As with Abraham and Sarah, so with Isaac and Rebekah: husband and wife are social actors motivated by a desire to fulfill individual aims while at the same time operating within the prescribed boundaries of the family system.

by conflict: brother against brother and husband against wife.[10]
From the previous cycle of stories, with its focus on the relationship between father and son, a shift occurs in this narrative cycle
to the relationship between kin, in general, and between brothers,
specifically.[11]

Genesis 26:1-33

Genesis 26:1-33 provides fundamental information about family
life in ancient Israel, especially that part of the narrative that recounts the adventures of Isaac and Rebekah when they dwell in
the land of the Philistines ruled by Abimelech. When we connect
the details of this pericope with those of Gen 12:10—13:1 and 20:1-
18 and then connect the passage with its immediate context, some
salient points emerge. The obvious difference between this story
and the other two so-called wife-sister tales is that in their travels
to a foreign land husband and wife are never separated from each
other—despite the fact that Isaac calls Rebekah his sister (v. 7).[12]
The king of the Philistines only later discovers that Isaac and Rebekah are not related to each other as brother and sister when he
spots them involved in apparent sexual activity; whatever they
are doing is enough to let Abimelech know that the two are actually husband and wife.[13] Ultimately, nothing even potentially
threatening happens to Rebekah, despite the use of the wife-sister
subterfuge. In this story, it is a ruse in name only. Some detail of
this story demanded that Rebekah's morality not be threatened
and the disruption of her marriage to Isaac not be attempted.
The other two accounts of a patriarch and a matriarch, Abraham

---

10. The family loyalties established here have fundamental importance for
future family politics and defensive strategies. They determine the entire course
of the Rebekah cycle. Cf. Westermann, who argues that the purpose of Gen
25:27-34 lies elsewhere; he concludes, "It is told to make people laugh" (*Promises*,
79).

11. Ibid., 75.

12. One problem with R. Polzin's analysis of the so-called wife-sister stories
is that it fails to explain why in this narrative there is only "potential adultery"
(" 'The Ancestress of Israel in Danger' in Danger," *Semeia* 3 [1975] 87).

13. In v. 8 of this story we encounter another piel form of the root *ṣḥq*; in this
case, there is the wordplay *yiṣḥāq meṣaḥēq* (Isaac was fondling). For the argument
that this root in the piel verbal stem should be interpreted sexually, see chapter 2,
above.

and Sarah, in a similar situation would lead the reader to expect that Rebekah would have been taken into Abimelech's household for his personal sexual enjoyment. Thus, we must ask why she was not. What detail(s) distinguishes this episode from the two previous situations of seemingly the same circumstances?

The puzzle of Genesis 26 is solved when the story is interpreted within its larger narrative context. The most important feature that distinguishes 26 from 12 and 20 is that Rebekah has already secured her position in Isaac's household by providing him not only with one son—but with two sons! From the perspective of the final redactor, through the birth of Jacob and Esau, Rebekah establishes her place in Isaac's home. A woman's security rests on her relationships through sons, and Rebekah now dwells securely with her husband. Hence, she is not expendable to Isaac the way the barren Sarah was to her heirless husband Abraham. In both Genesis 12 and 20, Sarah had not fulfilled her procreative function as primary wife. This difference between Genesis 26 and the other two wife-sister stories suggests how firmly established a woman became in her husband's household once she bore him an heir.

Data from comparative kinship studies reveal that motherhood conferred social and cultural validation within the family unit. A woman served the interests of her husband's family, and her own interests as well, when she provided him with a son to carry on his lineage; how much more so when Rebekah bore two sons!

Because Rebekah has helped guarantee the continuity of Isaac's lineage, Isaac cannot ignore her interests. Unlike the situation of Sarah in Abraham's household, Rebekah is not the ultimate source of the generational discontinuity in Isaac's household—at least not in a negative sense. Her status as mother has firmly entrenched her in the household of Isaac.

A cross-disciplinary perspective illumines literary-critical judgments; reasons of social convention prevented the final redactor from moving beyond the bare bones of tradition in recounting this adventure in a foreign land.[14] The significance of the status of

---

14. Van Seters's failure to read these stories in their larger narrative context forces him to conclude, regarding Gen 26:8: "This solution by the author of story C, however, ultimately raises more problems than it solves." Later he remarks: "Such a lack of interest in the folktale theme can only be explained by suggesting that the author's interest is elsewhere. . . . The intention of the author is suggested

mother foreshadows the strength of Rebekah's influence in her favoritism toward Jacob. As the narrative cycle progresses, she will be responsible for assuring Jacob's security against the advances of Esau and for sending Jacob off to get a wife from the Terahite lineage. Rebekah manages to get Jacob into a position whereby he becomes Isaac's lineal heir.

In the concluding part of this chapter, Gen 26:12-33, Isaac and Abimelech quarrel over wealth. This conflict eventuates in the same result as the earlier conflicts between Abraham and Lot, and then Abraham and Abimelech, and as the later ones between Jacob and Laban, and finally Jacob and Esau. What strikes our attention here is that the strife over wells occurs after Rebekah has had children and secured her place in her husband's family; earlier Abraham fought with the same foreign ruler over the same wells immediately after the birth of Isaac had secured Sarah's place in the family household. The connection between progeny and wealth becomes clear[15] from the stories in Genesis. Wealth always seems to bring conflict followed by covenant making, leading to separation.[16] Increase in family property leads to strife over material possessions, which raises questions of inheritance. The more children a man has, the more the conflict increases. Earlier, because Lot and Abram had no progeny at the time of their conflict, the two parted company with no need for a covenant to guarantee their future peaceful relationship.[17]

---

instead in the opening remark in which he directly parallels Isaac's life with that of Abraham. It seems to be an artificial tradition about Isaac based directly on the traditions about Abraham" (J. van Seters, *Abraham in History and Tradition* [New Haven: Yale Univ. Press, 1975] 179–80, 183). The bluntness of this episode is taken by many to indicate that this is the oldest of the wife-sister stories; see, for example, R. Kilian, *Die vorpriesterlichen Abrahams-Überlieferungen literarkritisch und traditionsgeschichtlich untersucht* (BBB 24; Bonn: P. Hanstein, 1966) 214; M. Noth, *A History of Pentateuchal Traditions* (Englewood Cliffs, N.J.: Prentice-Hall, 1972) 105; G. von Rad, *Genesis* (OTL; Philadelphia: Westminster, 1972) 271. Koch interprets this same bluntness to mean that it is the most recent of the three texts (K. Koch, *The Growth of the Biblical Tradition: The Form-Critical Method* [New York: Charles Scribner's Sons, 1969] 125).

15. See Polzin, "Ancestress of Israel," 81–98.

16. On these covenants, see D. McCarthy, "Three Covenants in Genesis," *CBQ* 26 (1964) 179–89. For a discussion of the relationship between 21:22-34 and 26:12-33, see van Seters, *Abraham in History*, 183–91.

17. On territorial strife, see Westermann, *Promises*, 65–68.

Genesis 26:34—28:9

Having already established in 25:27-34 that one of the requirements for being one's father's heir is possession of the family birthright, the Rebekah cycle moves forward to describe further conditions for assuming the position of heir. It appears that the father's blessing is important when he designates his lineal heir, and this blessing is one focus of 25:27-34.[18] The blessing is so important that Rebekah successfully arranges to reverse the birth order of her two sons. Consequently, Jacob receives the blessing that Isaac had originally intended to bestow upon Esau. The narrator stresses the alignment between parents and sons: Isaac speaks to Esau as his son (27:1; see 27:5) while Rebekah speaks to Jacob as her son (27:6, 8, 13). Although the pattern developed here of each parent working for his or her interests through a favorite son has already been established in 25:28, the implications of this favoritism are now fully described.

Moreover, I believe that a further requirement for being deemed heir is highlighted in the present text. This unit actually begins with the information included in the end of the prior chapter, Gen 26:34. Here the narrator informs the reader that he who will follow in his father's genealogy as heir must have the proper wife—that is, a woman from the patrilineage of Terah.[19] This is the third sine qua non for being reckoned the father's lineal heir. Hence, the topic of the importance of having an appropriate wife serves as the framework for the unit 26:34—28:9.

Information about the Hittite women to whom Esau was wed (26:34) seems initially to be of little importance. As if to suggest

---

18. On the father's blessing, see E. A. Speiser, "I Know Not the Day of My Death," *JBL* 84 (1955) 252-56. See T. L. Thompson (*The Historicity of the Patriarchal Narratives: The Quest for the Historical Abraham* [BZAW 133; Berlin: de Gruyter, 1974] 285-93), who concludes regarding this text: "And so we are not dealing here with the inheritance of property, but rather the determination of destiny. Destiny once established is irreversible" (293).

19. See Fishbane, "Composition and Structure," 25 n. 38. Fishbane notes that information regarding Esau's marriages frames the events in chapter 27. He correctly argues that the subject of Esau's Hittite wife in 26:34 can be read as the pretext for Rebekah's actions in 27:5-17, just as 27:46 provides the pretext for 28:1-5, and that Esau's taking of further wives in 28:6-9 to please his parents reflects this concern for "an appropriate wife." However, it is curious that, in defining the boundaries of the present unit, Fishbane chooses to begin it at 27:1—not 26:34. He does argue that the pericope ends at 28:9.

that the material could not be accounted for, and therefore was
suppressed, the redactor appears to have placed it in an obscure
point in the text. But in a body of literature primarily interested
in genealogical progression, information on marriage choices becomes highly significant. Who but the men and women involved
in these marriages are responsible for perpetuating the family
lineage? That Esau married outside the direct line of Israelites suggests that 26:34-35 describes events that will make it impossible
for Esau to have a place in the Terahite genealogy. The narrator's
report that Esau's Hittite wives made life bitter for Rebekah and
Isaac provides us with further data regarding marriage choices
appropriate for the heir to Isaac's vertical lineage.[20]

When Rebekah was first introduced into the genealogy of
Abraham (Genesis 24), she served as a source of exchange between two households, the one into which she was born and the
one to which she would go.[21] This is the perspective of structural
anthropology. Although Rebekah is asked directly whether she
is willing to be given in marriage, the implication is, based on
the gifts given to her household, that her brother (and father?)
wanted and expected her to accede to the agreement in order that
they might benefit materially from the arrangement.[22] Thus, in
theory, Rebekah had the freedom to refuse the marriage offer, but
in practice there would have been economic pressures for her not
to do so. Furthermore, the gifts Rebekah receives from Abraham's

20. Fishbane ("Composition and Structure," 35) comments on the importance
of ethnic purity for the perpetuation of the generations. From the household
economics perspective, one could argue that wives from outside the lineage are
a potential threat to the interests of their husbands' households if social custom
upholds their right to remain loyal to their fathers' concerns. "The basic dilemma
of the agnatic group is to deal with the anomalous presence of those people who
are in the group but not of it.... Domestic functions are the province of those
people lacking in inherent loyalty and solidarity—its attached women" (B. S.
Denich, "Sex and Power in the Balkans," *Woman, Culture, and Society* [ed. M. Z.
Rosaldo and L. Lamphere; Stanford, Calif.: Stanford Univ. Press, 1974] 251).

21. See K. R. Andriolo ("Myth and History: A General Model and Its Application to the Bible," *American Anthropologist* 83 [1981] 270, 278 n. 15) for additional
examples of biblical women as both objects of exchange and agents of change. It
is curious that when discussing the figure of Sarah, Andriolo neglects to mention
that the matriarch was an agent of change when she replaced Ishmael with Isaac
as Abraham's heir.

22. See R. G. D. Andrade ("Sex Differences and Cultural Institutions," *The
Development of Sex Differences* [ed. E. E. Maccoby; Stanford: Stanford Univ. Press,
1966] 173–203) on marriage refusal—with its attendant loss of gifts—as a source
of a daughter's/sister's power over her kin.

servant in order to entice her to marry Isaac contribute to her indirect dowry. They provide the economic basis for her marriage to Isaac. However, having moved into a new household and having established herself in it through motherhood, Rebekah no longer functions as an object of exchange between families. She is now an agent of change of status for her sons. In both contexts, she appears as a social actor consciously concerned to act in her own best interests.

That Rebekah would want to further the cause of Jacob, the son destined to be Isaac's heir, and thereby bind him to her in loyalty parallels the bond between Sarah and Isaac; but that she actually served her own interests by agreeing to marry Isaac in the first place needs to be emphasized. Rebekah's decision appears to be a carefully calculated one. If she had not assented, her own family might have found fit means for punishing her for having deprived them of the gifts that Abraham's servant brought for the prospective bride and her family. Further, cross-cultural data on family life emphasize that individual actions are typically motivated by group interests. Rebekah's actions benefit her father's household.

Then, while Rebekah is a member of Isaac's household, her treatment of Jacob benefits her own interests. It appears that in Genesis 27 she works shrewdly on his behalf because of Yahweh's words to her in Gen 25:23. Knowing already which of her two sons is to be next in line in Isaac's lineage, Rebekah changes the natural birth order of her sons by tricking Isaac into blessing Jacob instead of Esau. As argued above, Rebekah is motivated in her actions by the idea that the loyalty she will win from Jacob will insure her place in Isaac's household even after his death. Thus, Rebekah's apparently idiosyncratic behavior is intended to serve not only Jacob's interests but also her own. She "runs interference"[23] between the men in the household to shape the family according to her own and Yahweh's plan for them, and to guarantee her future. Ultimately, all the men in the family move according to the designs she has for them. At this point in the Rebekah cycle, they are all pawns in her game.[24]

---

23. This concept is borrowed from B. L. Chiñas, *The Isthmus Zapotecs: Women's Roles in Cultural Context* (New York: Holt, Rinehart and Winston, 1973). For examples of this principle, see 102–8.

24. Is it because the narrative cycle so immediately legitimates Rebekah's position in the household that she is quickly presented arranging family matters?

Cross-cultural analysis of the division of power in the family underscores the necessity of the blessing of Isaac in order that Rebekah's attempt to reverse the birth order of Jacob and Esau can be realized.[25] Both parents must be involved in the scheme, even if the husband is not a knowing party to the plan. Each is circumscribed by the other in exercising power.

With Jacob in possession of the family birthright and the family blessing, he appears to hold all the necessary credentials for assuming the role of lineal heir to his father. With this situation sketched out, the story shifts back to the topic of non-Israelite wives in Gen 27:46—the same subject that served as the focal point of discussion in the opening verses of this unit. Rebekah returns to the matter of Esau's foreign wives, motivated partially by her fear that Esau's anger may prompt him to kill Jacob, and thus deprive Rebekah of her security in the family that this son represents to her, after the death of Isaac (27:41-45). Using the bitterness that these women have caused her as the pretext for persuading Isaac to send Jacob to Paddan-aram to find a wife, Rebekah is able to remove Jacob from the path of the wrath of Esau, and avoid bloodshed—at least for the time being.[26] Rebekah, the one responsible for placing Jacob in this danger from Esau, now saves him from the repercussions of her scheme.

However, the bitterness that Rebekah and Isaac experience because of Esau's marriages suggests that more lies behind Rebekah's insistence that Jacob return to Paddan-aram for a wife than the search for an acceptable spouse. We must weigh the pos-

---

Sarah would seem to be no less deliberate in her attempts to secure for herself what she desires; yet her barrenness appears to limit how boldly or conspicuously she may act. For the argument that the difference in character development can be explained on the basis of extended narrative and the retreat of God in the Jacob stories, see R. L. Cohn, "Narrative Structure and Canonical Perspective in Genesis," *JSOT* 25 (1983) 10.

25. For the conclusion, "Female accomplishments need formal accreditation by men," see Andriolo, "Myth and History," 275. According to Andriolo, another example of the interrelationship of the roles of men and women in exactly this manner may be found in Genesis 38. Not until Judah acknowledges that he is the father of Tamar's child can her status as a mother be legitimated in the society.

26. Source critics divide 27:1-45 (J) from 27:46—28:9 (P) and argue that the original rationale for Rebekah's insistence that Jacob leave is her fear of the harm that will come to Jacob from Esau. Gen 27:46—28:9 is seen as a later insertion into the original text. See, for example, von Rad, *Genesis*, 279, 281–82. As the text now stands, both Rebekah's fear for the safety of Jacob and her concern that he find the proper wife serve as motives for her actions.

sibility that only through his marriage to a member of his own family line will Jacob be able to take his place in the lineal genealogy of his father, Isaac.[27] Esau's second marriage—an attempt to reverse the unpleasantness caused to his parents by his first marriage to Hittite women—characterizes a man desperately trying to do that which will bring merit to him in his parents' eyes so that he may have a chance at being considered his father's heir. It is not without irony that in this desperation Esau chooses Mahalath, who is a daughter of Ishmael, for his next marriage (v. 9). The line of Ishmael, of course, is not the line chosen to carry on Abraham's Israelite lineage. In effect, through his second marriage, Esau only further removes himself from any possibility of being considered his father's heir. Mahalath is an inappropriate wife for an Israelite son because she is not descended through the vertical lineage.

Thus, the resolution of heirship questions becomes further complicated. Esau, the son presumed to be his father's heir, has theoretically been eliminated as his father's choice for an heir through loss of birthright, blessing, and the wrong marriage choices. The son who might not have been socially sanctioned as heir, the younger son, Jacob, has already acquired two out of the three credentials seemingly necessary to be lineal heir to Isaac.

The story now dramatically advances through new developments in the generation of Isaac's descendants. As Jacob sets out on a trip to his mother's homeland, it appears that circumstances have converged so that he will secure soon the final requisite necessary for movement into his father's Israelite lineage, just as in the Sarah-Hagar cycle Isaac was ready to be his father's heir only after he acquired a wife from his parent's homeland. Again, in order for a boy to become a man not only must he take a bride— he must also take the "proper" bride if he is to be recognized as heir to his father. In the case of Jacob, the arguments of his mother, Rebekah, make it possible for her favorite son to make the journey

---

27. While Rebekah takes personal responsibility for arranging that Jacob receives his father's blessing and the appropriate wife, it is unclear whether she was instrumental in Jacob obtaining Esau's birthright. But it would appear improper to suggest that Jacob had designs from the outset on being his father's heir and that obtaining the birthright was the first step in his larger plan. Verses 11-12 make it clear that he is troubled by his mother's scheme; he worries that it will backfire and that instead of a blessing he will receive a curse. Yet without birthright, blessing, and proper wife, Jacob cannot assume the status of lineal heir to Isaac.

that will allow him to enter marriage with his proper bride. Rebekah is a social actor responsible for resolving the disequilibrium in the generation of Isaac's descendants caused by the presence of two sons—both of whom might become heirs.

The tension between these two sons is emphasized throughout this entire episode by the preponderance of family terms and the repetition of the fact that Jacob is Rebekah's son while Esau is Isaac's son. The story is one of a family divided against itself as each individual works to further his or her own interests. And yet there is a delicate balance maintained despite this family strife. Family fission does not occur. Jacob leaves, temporarily it seems, to avoid total family fission. Rebekah, the only woman in the story, controls the household in the meantime by working through one of the men—her son Jacob—without the full awareness of her husband, Isaac, and his favorite son, Esau.

Genesis 28:10-22

Through the inclusion of the unit Gen 28:10-22, the narrator provides an additional clue for interpreting the developing events in the family of Isaac. This episode, recounting Jacob's meeting with Yahweh in a dream at Bethel, may be understood to provide divine sanction to the plan initiated by Rebekah to make Jacob the heir of Isaac.[28] What has only been hinted at in the Rebekah cycle— that the legal heir to the father's lineal genealogy must possess birthright, blessing, and proper spouse—is now confirmed. The addition of Yahweh's blessing to Jacob's growing list of good fortune furnishes the final stamp of approval needed to make him heir in Isaac's genealogy.

---

28. See Andriolo, "Structural Analysis," 1668: Rebekah's plan involves "the process by which the goal of competition is achieved. In the Jacob-Esau story this process consists of three steps, proceeding from the lowest to the highest level of recognition. First, the agreement of the brother is gained: the elder brother sells his firstborn's privilege to the younger brother in exchange for something to eat. Secondly, in the form of the firstborn's blessing, the recognition of the father is gained through deception; the younger brother goes to the father pretending to be the elder brother. Thirdly, God gives his recognition of the younger brother's new status, after matters are decided on the human level; he blesses Jacob with the promise of descendants."

Genesis 29:1–32:1

The pericope in 29:1—32:1 (Hebrew) dramatically advances the plot of the story to the point at which Jacob possesses wives, children, and property. He acquires these through his association with the household of his mother's brother Laban. At the same time, these developments in Jacob's life add further problems to the ensuing genealogy. They foreshadow the next narrative cycle, which focuses on the question: Which of Jacob's wives will produce his heir?[29]

In many respects, the course of events during Jacob's stay with Laban parallels events that occurred while Jacob dwelt in the house of his father, Isaac.[30] Laban's role in advancing the interests of his daughters may be compared to Rebekah's arranging the fate of her sons. From a literary perspective, brother and sister have parallel functions. Mother and father exercise equal power over their offspring. Each parent uses deceit in order to further the cause of the offspring who is seemingly the underdog in the matter of sibling rivalry. The actions of Rebekah and Laban become the source of literary tension, while the narrative works to resolve the competition between younger and older sibling. And Jacob's role vis-à-vis his two wives is analogous to that of Isaac earlier vis-à-vis his two sons: both men confirm recognition of the reversal of the relationship between the siblings. Isaac blesses Jacob, and later Jacob becomes Leah's husband.

The competition between Rachel and Leah (one barren, the other not) is reminiscent of the competition between Sarah and Hagar (one barren, the other not).[31] All four women work to le-

---

29. For the argument that this is a matrilateral, cross-cousin marriage—that is, Jacob weds the daughters of his mother's brother—see M. E. Donaldson, "Kinship Theory in the Patriarchal Narratives: The Case of the Barren Wife," *JAAR* 49 (1981) 87–98; and R. A. Oden, "Jacob as Father, Husband, and Nephew: Kinship Studies and the Patriarchal Narratives," *JBL* 102 (1983) 189–205. The problems with this line of reasoning have been addressed in chapter 1, above.

30. Andriolo makes an ingenious argument for the symmetry between the behavior and circumstances of Jacob and Esau, on the one hand, and Rachel and Leah, on the other hand. The basic component in these two sets of sibling rivalry is a desire to be parent to the individual through whom the lineage will pass. See her complete analysis in "Structural Analysis," 1667–68.

31. Despite the present tension between the two sisters, Rachel and Leah later unite in their common interest to leave Laban's household when they feel he has deprived them of their inheritance. In this situation, women work together

gitimate their places in the family household through their ability
to provide their husband with an heir. In the case of these four
women who are presented as two pairs of individuals in competition with each other, the author creates fully developed characters.
They breathe narrative life. (This contrasts with the case of Lot's
two daughters.) The crisis presented by barrenness would seem
to be implicit in the matter of character development.

While the brothers Jacob and Esau compete for the position of
heir, the two sisters Leah and Rachel fight for a place of honor in
Jacob's lineage. Each woman desires to be the mother of the son
through whom her husband's line will continue. The Sarah-Hagar
cycle has already prepared the reader for the problem: when a
man has two sons, only one may be recognized as his lineal heir.
But the competition between Sarah and Hagar differs from that
between Leah and Rachel in that in the former case only one of
the women is the husband's legal wife; the other is a secondary
co-wife. Once they both bear sons, the legal wife has an authority
unavailable to a servant. However, since both Leah and Rachel are
legal wives of Jacob, an arrangement of sororal polygyny, we do
not know which woman should be recognized as the mother of
Jacob's heir. Moreover, Jacob's love for Rachel (29:18, 20, 30) raises
the possibility that emotions, rather than just status, will become
the basis for the husband-wife relationship.

Jacob's marriage to Leah and Rachel, both of whom are
deemed appropriate wives (as Gen 29:4 makes clear, they are from
the lineage of Nahor, the brother of Terah) for the man who will
be his father's lineal heir, would appear to secure his role in the
Terahite genealogy of Isaac. However, while these marriages secure the lineal genealogy for the time being, they also introduce
a source of potential disharmony in Jacob's household because of
the equal social standing of Rachel and Leah.[32] Once Rachel and
Leah bear children, the situation of sororal polygyny raises heirship questions for the future direction of the Terahite lineage. And

because it is in their interest to do so. Conflict and cooperation derive from the
circumstances in which they find themselves.

32. Although, due to Rachel's barrenness, they are initially unequal. Yet this
inequality due to procreative dysfunction is offset by the inequality of Jacob's
affections for his two wives. The barren wife is the more loved wife. See 1 Samuel
1 for a similar, though not identical, case. The rivalry between the two sisters
remains the central dynamic of the story. Even the names given to their children
reflect this bitter conflict.

we must also consider the sons borne to Jacob by his wives' maids, Bilhah and Zilpah, as competitors for a position in this lineal genealogy. Bilhah and Zilpah appear to be the direct dowry Laban gave to his daughters when they married (29:24, 29).[33]

Additional literary confirmation that Rachel and Leah are potential proper spouses for the heir to Isaac's line derives from the story told in 29:1-15. When Jacob arrives at Paddan-aram he chances to meet Rachel at a well; this literary detail reminds the reader of Abraham's servant's journey back to the homeland to find a bride for Isaac. The servant meets Rebekah, the woman who becomes Isaac's wife, at a well. Based on these prior events (Gen 24:11-27), one would expect that the woman Jacob encounters at the well is the one appropriate to be the proper wife.[34] But again, in Jacob's case the situation has been complicated due to the existence of two daughters and the local custom, or so according to Laban, of marrying off the elder daughter before giving away the younger one in marriage.[35]

Cross-cultural anthropological data help us understand the meaning of the conflict and cooperation between Rachel and Leah once they are both married to Jacob. Each works to win his favor by bearing him children. If we maintain this anthropological perspective and recognize the two sisters as social agents who act out of self-interest, then we recognize their behavior as an indication

---

33. The text specifically states that both Zilpah and Bilhah were Laban's maids before they were given to Leah and Rachel as their maids. Although Zilpah and Bilhah are referred to as *šipḥâ* (maidservant), the lowest status of maid, both before and after they bear children, the term *'āmâ* (handmaid) also occurs in the text in a somewhat inconsistent manner. For example, in 30:3 Rachel refers to Bilhah as her *'āmâ* when she tells Jacob to have children with her, but in 30:4 the narrator labels Bilhah a *šipḥâ*. The pattern appears to be that when the narrator reports events, *šipḥâ* is the preferred terminology, but in direct speech *'āmâ* is used. See the discussion of these terms in chapter 2 n. 55, above.

34. J. G. Williams, "The Beautiful and the Barren: Conventions in Biblical Type-Scenes," *JSOT* 17 (1980) 109.

35. Is this a form of rebuke directed at Jacob for having deceived his own father by pretending that the younger son is the older son? Jacob, the younger, claimed to be the elder; Leah, the elder, claimed to be the younger. This literature demonstrates the importance of the trickster role in Genesis; it is a role open to both men and women for achieving their goals. See Fishbane, "Composition and Structure," 30. For an analysis of Jacob the trickster from the perspective of folklore studies, see S. Niditch, *Underdogs and Tricksters: A Prelude to Biblical Folklore* (San Francisco: Harper & Row, 1987) 70–125. See the essays in *Reasoning with the Foxes: Female Wit in a World of Male Power*, ed. J. C. Exum and J. W. H. Bos, *Semeia* 42 (1988) for more on trickery in the Hebrew Bible.

of conflict in Jacob's household. From a cross-cultural perspective, we can analyze quarreling, jealousy, and anger as signs of Rachel's and Leah's attempts to control their situations and exercise power over them.

Rachel and Leah's quarrels (and the earlier ones between Sarah and Hagar) derive from conflictual situations in which the interests of one woman are pitted against those of another. In such contexts, one means for women to exercise power is through their arguments. Their actions are their acts of resistance. As one anthropologist has stated it, "Where there is resistance, there is power."[36] Rachel's and Leah's behavior toward each other reflects strife in Jacob's household over uncertain genealogical progression. This behavior can be viewed as an attempt to subvert family power structures. Cross-cultural data on women's resistance to social situations in which they feel exploited indicate that women's quarrels in the Bible square with a pattern of behavior (namely, quarreling) that appears to have a common meaning.[37] In this case, the disruptive behavior represents each woman's attempt to exert self-interest by seeing to it that her sister will not be Jacob's primary wife, despite the fact that from the perspective of the final redactor both women are recognized as legal wives.

The cross-cultural data on women's resistance to patrilineal power structures shed new light on women's argumentative, jealous behavior in the Genesis stories. Quarreling, as an expression of women's resistance, becomes a reaction against exploitation by men in situations in which only one woman will be victorious. One woman attempts to gain power over the other through her disruptive behavior. Women's words represent an attempt to subvert the power controlling women's reproduction. The most frequent context for such conflict between women occurs at that stage in the family life cycle when women are expected to bear children, which is precisely the life cycle stage in Genesis about which we have the

---

36. L. Abu-Lughod, "The Romance of Resistance: Tracing Transformations of Power through Bedouin Women," *Beyond the Second Sex: New Directions in the Anthropology of Gender* (ed. P. Sanday and R. G. Goodenough; Philadelphia: Univ. of Pennsylvania Press, 1990) 314–15.

37. Proverbs contains five references to women's quarrels and to the unpleasantness that comes to the family because of them (Prov 19:13; 21:9; 21:19; 25:24; 27:15). The question is whether men or women are the speakers of these sayings. The proverbs can either be expressions of men's fears or of women's power.

most information. In fact, the names of the children of Rachel and
Leah are comments on their marriages and on childbearing.

In claiming that quarreling is an expression of resistance, we
need to recognize that such behavior may be socially sanctioned.
Consequently, while women resist exploitation, they also support
the situation they resist. Rachel and Leah continually quarrel with
each other over childbearing even as they attempt to bring forth as
many offspring as they possibly can. In other words, resistance at
one level may entangle an individual in a power web at another
level. The forms that resistance takes help us to understand the
power dynamics of the social context in which women in Genesis
find themselves.

What distinguishes the two genders is that men attempt to
gain power whereas women attempt to resist it. In Genesis the
behavior of men in conflict appears less an act of resistance and
more a man's attempt to displace his opponent from the scene. In
other words, one man must deprive another man of something
in order for the first man to succeed.[38] Abraham expels Ishmael;
Jacob cheats Esau out of his birthright and tricks Isaac into giving
him a blessing; and, as we soon will see, Laban cheats Jacob out of
his wages (31:7); Jacob outwits Laban for his flock; and ultimately
Joseph's brothers sell him into slavery. There are, of course, other
examples of similar behavior outside of Genesis.[39] The resolution
of conflict between Abram and Lot in Genesis 13 is striking because it is an exception to this expectation. As we have already
observed, rather than compete with each other, the two separate
and go their own ways when they both become so wealthy that
the land cannot support them together. In this case, one does not
need to displace the other because separation brings both Abram
and Lot enough land to satisfy their desires.

While instances of conflict in Genesis may be analyzed from
a literary-critical perspective as means of providing suspense in
the story, kinship studies demonstrate that conflictual behavior

---

38. Andriolo, "Myth and History," 271.

39. I have confined my examples to individuals bound to each other by kinship
or marriage. One thinks otherwise of the conflict between Abraham and Abimelech in Gen 21:22-34. For examples of cooperation between women when their
fertility is not at issue, the cooperation between the Hebrew midwives Siphrah
and Puah in Exod 1:15-21 is instructive. Also, there is the cooperation of pharaoh's
daughter with the mother and sister of the baby boy she rescues in Exodus 2.

reflects the central dynamics of family life. For example, the competition between Jacob, on the one hand, and Laban and his sons, on the other hand (30:25—31:2), suggests that the multiple-family household of Laban[40] is an economic unit, though not a common productive unit—that is, each unit is contributing to a common fund, and benefiting from it, with an awareness of differing sizes of contribution. Consequently, Laban is aware that if he grants Jacob's request and allows his son-in-law to leave, the family income will suffer (30:27). Laban's sons realize that if Jacob leaves with all he has acquired from the family cattle, the size of their inheritance will be seriously diminished (31:1). It is in the interest of Laban and his sons to avoid the family fission that would result from Jacob's departure. However, from Jacob's point of view, only by leaving Laban's household will it be possible to build up his own family unit. Each man tries to assert himself over the other in order to maintain his wealth.

After Rachel and Leah encourage Jacob that this is appropriate action, and that they are willing to leave with him (31:4-16), Jacob finally decides to return to his homeland. The women agree to depart because of their complaint against Laban: part of their father's inheritance that belongs to them has been stolen by him. Based on cross-cultural investigation of marriage transactions, we can infer that Rachel and Leah may be speaking of either direct dowry, gifts from their father, or indirect dowry, gifts from Jacob, or both. As indicated above, Genesis 29 reports that Leah and Rachel received the maidservants Zilpah and Bilhah as direct dowry from Laban. However, because Jacob worked for Laban in exchange for his wives, an indirect dowry may not have been given. Based on their remark in 31:15, the two sisters feel entitled to some material compensation from Laban in light of all that their father gained through Jacob's work. This would be in lieu of an indirect dowry. Rachel and Leah may also have been deprived of a direct dowry from Laban—other than each daughter's maid—because they remained as members of their father's household after their marriages.[41]

The harmony between Rachel and Leah stands in direct contrast to the opposition that earlier separated them. At this stage

---

40. I assume that Laban and his sons have wives.
41. Westbrook, *Property and the Family*, 156–58.

in their family life, their common interests unite them with each other and with Jacob against Laban. Through childbearing, each woman has secured a place in her husband's household and thinks there is much to be gained by severing the relationship with her father.

Fission occurs in Laban's household when his son-in-law and daughters leave over material possessions. The blow is severe to Laban, and he sets out in pursuit of Jacob, Rachel, Leah, their children, and their cattle. Laban's kinsmen accompany him to protect his interests, just as earlier kinship obligations bound Abraham to come to Lot's rescue (Genesis 14).

When Laban and his kinfolk meet up with Jacob and his family, the former tells the latter that he is offended because Jacob left without the proper farewell. In addition, Laban claims that Jacob fled with what rightfully belongs to Laban, and that he would have sent the family off with fanfare if only he had been given the chance. Laban's protests about departure protocol notwithstanding, the conflict between the two men really revolves around matters of property. The only specific complaint Laban lodges against Jacob is that Laban's household gods, his teraphim, have disappeared in the company of the departing group.[42]

After Rachel's theft of her father's household gods eludes Laban's search for them,[43] Laban and Jacob formalize the family

---

42. Although it is no longer possible to determine the significance of the teraphim that Rachel stole from her father, it is interesting that one commentator argues these gods were important in settling matters of inheritance; see A. E. Draffkorn, "Ilâni/Elohim," *JBL* 76 (1957) 216–24. In that case, Rachel's actions appear to be motivated by her earlier claim (31:14) that Laban had deprived Rachel and Leah of their rightful inheritance. In stealing her father's teraphim, Rachel is settling Laban's debt to her and Leah. On the possibility that the teraphim should be associated with the religious practices of women in ancient Israel, see P. A. Bird, "Israelite Religion and the Faith of Israel's Daughters: Reflections on Gender and Religious Definition," *The Bible and the Politics of Exegesis* (ed. D. Jobling et al.; Cleveland: Pilgrim, 1991) 102. N. Jay argues that the theft of the teraphim reflects Rachel's attempt to control descent through women (*Throughout Your Generations Forever: Sacrifice, Religion, and Paternity* [Chicago and London: Univ. of Chicago Press, 1992] 107).

43. Not without significance for understanding family roles is the fact that Rachel so easily eludes Laban's search by claiming, "the way of women is upon me" (31:25). We must consider the possibility that this is a prevarication guaranteed to get Rachel what she wants: the household gods! To those who would ask, How can we know whether she was telling the truth or not?, the point is precisely that we cannot. Based on family custom, Rachel knew how to keep Laban away from her with an excuse that no man would check on. Although it is impossible

fission and their kinship relationship with a covenant witnessed
by their kinsmen. As part of the agreement, Jacob swears that he
will take no other wives besides Rachel and Leah (31:50). Upon
the completion of this treaty, two separate family units are finally
established.

Genesis 32:2-3

Having acquired the final credential (wives from the lineage of
Terah) needed to be his father's heir, Jacob hopes to return to
Canaan and take his place in the genealogy of Isaac and thereby
acquire his father's land and inheritance. From a literary perspective, Jacob's need to guarantee his security against the potential
wrath of his rival heir, Esau, parallels the moment in the prior
narrative cycle when Sarah arranges for the safety of Isaac in the
presence of his rival heir, Ishmael (Gen 21:8-14). The brief incident recounted in 32:2-3 may be taken as an example of divine
approval of the chain of events in Jacob's life thus far and as a
guarantee against Esau in the future. God apparently endorses Jacob as Isaac's lineal heir after he acquires proper wives for himself
from his mother's family in Paddan-aram.

Genesis 32:4—33:17

Jacob moves further into position as his father's heir in the episode in 32:4—33:17. Here he returns to Canaan with the wives,
sons, and property needed to supplement the birthright and the
blessing he had acquired earlier. In particular, the unit advances
the Rebekah cycle to the point that Jacob maneuvers a working relationship with his brother Esau. The two brothers are ultimately

---

to know what the ancient Israelite knew about conception and pregnancy, the
fact is that later on in the journey, Rachel gives birth to Benjamin (35:16-18). The
text does not indicate how much longer after they originally set out this event
occurred; but possibly the notice of Benjamin's birth is the narrator's means for
informing the reader that Rachel was lying all along. To be sure, this is only con-
jectural, but it is definitely worth considering. Jay connects the menstrual blood
in this story and the sacrificial blood in 31:54 to attempts to resolve issues of
conflict between descent from mothers and descent from fathers; she reads this
as a concern in the putative E writer (*Throughout Your Generations*, 107–8).

free of sibling rivalry. Through the servile attitude he feigns toward Esau, Jacob appears secure in the knowledge that he is presently safe from the vengeance of Esau.

The details of the story (32:22-32) of the change of name Jacob undergoes at the Jabbok may be interpreted as further divine approval of the incidents relating to Jacob's plan to secure his position as heir against the earlier rival claims of Esau. Possibly this incident occurs when it does to express the narrator's approval of Jacob as lineal heir to Isaac.[44]

As the cycle moves toward its conclusion and settles the matter of disharmony in the family genealogy, family relational terms, previously used so frequently, more or less drop from the text. As opposed to the prior texts with their heavy emphasis on terms defining how individuals are related to each other as kin, in this story Jacob and Esau are presented as individuals working to break the ties that bind them as brothers and to emerge as autonomous characters with their own separate fates.

Genesis 33:18–34:31

Now that we have seen in the story of Jacob's trip to Laban's household how and where Israelite men are expected to find proper women for marriage partners, the story of Dinah and Shechem in 33:18—34:31 addresses the question of appropriate spouses for Israelite women. Both 33:18—34:31 and 29:1—32:1 deal with the topic of social boundaries appropriate for Israelite marriages. Both arrive at the same conclusion: Israelites should not marry outside the circle of kinship reckoned through the patrilateral genealogy of Terah.

This narrative about Dinah's marriage is the counterpart of the

---

44. Studies of Gen 32:22-32 are legion. A novel explanation of why Jacob is the patriarch named Israel and why his name is changed at precisely this point in his narrative life is provided by Oden, "Jacob as Father," 202-3. He writes: "When Jacob marries his mother's brother's daughter, and when he is thereby forced to establish a relationship with his maternal uncle, a complete kinship system is described; and thus Israel properly speaking is born. Similarly, Israel is also first adequately defined, both externally and internally . . . , when the preceding linear genealogy becomes a segmented genealogy with Jacob's sons. In all cases, the decisive relationships are those established by the man who receives the name Israel" (202). However, see the critique of Oden in chapter 1, above.

one describing Esau's marriage to Canaanite women; only here, the story is told from the perspective of the status of the bride— and not the bridegroom. From a cross-cultural perspective, the primary concern in both cases is the effect of the marriage on the father of the Israelite family.[45] Marriage outside the kinship group breaks down family solidarity. The same interest was expressed earlier when, in Genesis 24, Abraham gave explicit instructions to his servant regarding who would be a fit wife for his son. The subject will arise again in the story of Judah and Tamar in Genesis 38. The obvious focus on the progression of the genealogy from father to son—with less attention on how the in-marrying spouse affects the mother of the household—would seemingly account for the centrality of the relationship between the spouse who marries into the family and the father-in-law of this new spouse.[46]

Just as Esau's marriage to foreign women was viewed in an unfavorable light, so too was the marriage of Dinah to Shechem. The latter marriage destroys lineage solidarity and deprives a member of the Terahite line of a potential wife. But while Esau was ultimately responsible for having made such marriages—the text gives no indication that his parents were consulted in this matter—when Dinah was married, Jacob consented to the union. All the negotiations for Dinah's marriage are carried out by men following the rules guiding the formalities of this agreement. (Not once in the entire story do we learn of Dinah's feelings about Shechem or of her reaction to the impending marriage.) Thus, it is Jacob himself who brings strife to the family when he agrees to allow the marriage of his daughter outside the appropriate circle of bridegrooms. Jacob's sons, however, object to the marriage for reasons relating to family honor; family honor appears linked to control of the sexuality of women. When Shechem violated the

---

45. In addition, cross-cultural studies suggest that when a woman marries inside her kinship group, there is greater likelihood that she will be treated well by her husband and his family than if she marries outside the group; see L. Holy, *Kinship, Honour and Solidarity* (Manchester: Manchester Univ. Press, 1989) 49–52. Moreover, as discussed in chapter 1, marriage outside the group has economic repercussions; family property passes outside kinship boundaries.

46. Contra von Rad, *Genesis*, 255, the concern is both to keep the lineage pure through contracting an appropriate marriage and to maintain continuous existence on the land; one without the other would remove both Isaac and Jacob from their places as their fathers' rightful heirs.

honor of Dinah, the honor and safety of her entire family were threatened. Anthropological studies suggest that men who are thought to be unable to control the sexual honor of their women are also thought to be unable to defend themselves against attacks from outsiders.[47] In an attempt to prove their ability to protect themselves, Simeon and Levi, two of Jacob's sons, show the sons of Shechem their power in a mass attack on the men of the city.[48] This killing will have future repercussions when the topic of Jacob's heir is addressed in the Rachel-Leah cycle.

For the present, Gen 33:18—34:31 supplements the Rebekah cycle by proving that Jacob has now learned the social boundaries for marriage for both himself and his sons and daughters. In addition, the episode illustrates that not only has Jacob secured his safety against the threat of Esau, he has also firmly entrenched himself in Canaan against the threat posed by the indigenous inhabitants. In all respects, the disharmony present in the generation of Isaac's sons is progressing toward a harmony reflecting the stable state of events in family life. As Jacob acquires the proper credentials for being Isaac's lineal heir, he matures in the knowledge necessary for that status. Thus, with the total stability of the family of Jacob in hand, the cycle of Isaac's life draws nearer to a close.[49]

---

47. On women's honor as a function of men's political vulnerability, see A. Abou-Zeid, "Honour and Shame among the Bedouins of Egypt," *Honour and Shame: The Values of Mediterranean Society* (ed. J. G. Peristany; Chicago: Univ. of Chicago Press, 1966) 245–57; J. A. Pitt-Rivers, *The Fate of Shechem or the Politics of Sex* (Cambridge Studies in Social Anthropology 19; Cambridge: Cambridge Univ. Press, 1977). One should also note the variation in concepts of honor and shame between one social class in ancient Israel and the next. Cf. Genesis 34 and 2 Samuel 13–14, two stories of the rape of a sister and the differing reactions to the situation by brothers and fathers.

48. Both Jacob and his sons are interested in their relationship with their neighbors, but they take different approaches. Jacob believes the marriage of Dinah and Shechem will keep the peace between their peoples, while his sons believe the proper relationship can result only from military might. Issues of honor among the small family prompt the brothers to assert themselves in a case of rape. T. J. Prewitt argues that the levirate law rule is the basis for the mass murder by Simeon and Levi; otherwise Dinah would have had to marry another man from the line of Hamor (Prewitt, *The Elusive Covenant* [Bloomington and Indianapolis: Indiana Univ. Press, 1990] 109).

49. Note that in Gen 33:19, Jacob buys a piece of land that will eventually serve as Joseph's burial ground (Josh 24:32).

Genesis 35:1-21

In 35:1-21, Jacob journeys from Shechem to Mamre by divine directive. Whatever else may underlie the text, it serves as further confirmation of Jacob's loyalty to God based on his position in his father's Israelite genealogy.[50]

The importance of the death of Rachel, the "barren" wife, upon the birth of Benjamin should be noted. Just as the other barren wife, Sarah, died her narrative death after fulfilling her procreative functions, so too does Rachel. Both women die prior to their husbands. It is significant that, as with Sarah, notice of Rachel's burial place is given. This is dissimilar from the situation regarding Rebekah and Leah, the fertile wives. The women who have overcome the problem of barrenness, which had once set them at such a disadvantage in their husbands' households, appear to be singled out for specific mention through the details of their burial.[51]

Genesis 35:22-29

Genesis 35:22-29, the account of Reuben, son of Leah, having sexual intercourse with Bilhah—his father's concubine and Rachel's maid—foreshadows the upcoming uncertainty on the resolution of heirship decisions in the next narrative cycle. The story prepares the reader for the possibility that the firstborn of Jacob's twelve sons will move into genealogical place as his father's lineal heir.[52] Thus, it may be that Reuben's actions are

---

50. On God's directive to Jacob in 35:2, see O. Keel, "Das Vergraben der 'fremden Götter' in Genesis XXXV 4b," *VT* 23 (1973) 305–36; E. Nielsen, "The Burial of the Foreign Gods," *ST* 8 (1954) 103–22.

51. See chapter 2, above. Jay interprets Rachel's death as fulfillment of the sentence Jacob pronounced earlier for the individual who stole Laban's teraphim (*Throughout Your Generations*, 108–9).

52. On the significance of this act, see Speiser, *Genesis*, 274. Cf. 2 Sam 3:6-8; 16:21-22; 1 Kgs 2:21-22. Contra Fishbane, "Composition and Structure," this text must be included within the Rebekah cycle. It parallels 25:7-11 as the conclusion to the narrative cycle. Both Gen 35:27-29 and Gen 25:7-11 report the death and burial of the heir to the Terahite lineage who was named in the genealogy that began the narrative cycle. Cf. L. R. Fisher, "The Patriarchal Cycles," *Orient and Occident: Essays Presented to Cyrus H. Gordon on the Occasion of His Sixty-Fifth*

prompted by some prerogative he believes belongs to the lineal heir.[53]

The question is: How would Reuben insure himself the status of lineal heir by having sexual intercourse with one of his father's secondary wives? In his desire to be lineal heir, he confronts the social norm that in cases of sororal polygyny all sons have an equal right to share in their father's patrilineal inheritance. The equal social status of their mothers guarantees this.[54] Rather than allowing for the possibility that all the sons of Leah and Rachel would inherit from Jacob after he dies, Reuben tries to become his father's lineal heir by having sexual intercourse with Bilhah. However, at this time the story does not clarify what Reuben's intentions were.[55] Nothing more is stated in 35:22b than that Jacob heard about what his son did. For the time being, Reuben's actions are legitimate within the social system because no one objects to them.[56]

Although the text does not tell us what precisely Jacob thought or did in response to the situation with Reuben, it does inform us that Bilhah is now Jacob's *pîlegeš*, his secondary wife, whereas previously the text labels her both as *'āmâ* (handmaid; 30:3) and *šipḥâ* (maidservant; 30:4). The term *pîlegeš* appears to carry a status higher than either *'āmâ* or *šipḥâ*.[57] Possibly the terminology

---

Birthday (ed. H. A. Hoffner; AOAT 22; Neukirchen-Vluyn: Neukirchener, 1973) 61.

53. See 1 Kgs 2:13-25. Adonijah's request that Abishag, David's mistress, become Adonijah's wife is understood by Solomon as a request for David's kingship and his kingdom. In this case, Reuben becomes like his father Jacob, a part of the Terahite lineage, by having sexual intercourse with Bilhah.

54. J. Goody, *The Orient, the Ancient and the Primitive: Systems of Marriage and the Family in the Pre-industrial Societies of Eurasia* (Cambridge: Cambridge Univ. Press, 1990) 350.

55. It is not clear to me on what grounds Silberman can assert, "The narrative makes it clear that from Jacob's point of view the true heir is the elder son of the chosen wife, Rachel, i.e., Joseph. The author acquiesces in Jacob's fancy and removes the oldest son, Reuben, the apparent heir through the Bilhah episode" ("Listening to the Text," 23). Silberman's argument depends upon knowledge from hindsight. It seems to me, at this point, the text is ambiguous about the future of Jacob's lineage. Cf. von Rad, *Genesis*, 341: "The note is so brief and fragmentary that one can form no opinion about what is told in vs 21f."

56. R. Firth, "Some Principles of Social Organization," *Essays in Social Organization and Values* (London School of Economics Monographs on Social Anthropology 28; London: Athlone, 1964) 61.

57. This is the conclusion reached by K. Engelken (*Frauen im Alten Israel: Eine begriffsgeschichtliche und sozialrechtliche Studie zur Stellung der Frau im Alten Testa-*

switches at this point in the narrative because with the death of Rachel immediately before, the status of her handmaid becomes elevated in Jacob's household.

The story continues. Now that Jacob is firmly established in his role as lineal heir to his father, the Rebekah cycle can conclude with news of the death of Isaac. Jacob has all the credentials and has met all the requirements necessary to serve in this role in his father's lineage. Matters of lineage are emphasized at the conclusion to this narrative cycle when we are informed that Jacob returns to the place where his Terahite ancestors Abraham and Isaac lived. Isaac can now die to the story because he has an heir from the Terahite lineage to solve the problem of family disharmony; this is the heir whose family life and descendants will provide the focus of the third and final cycle of narratives in the family stories of Genesis.

Finally, with the news of Isaac's death, the conclusion to the Rebekah cycle parallels the end of the Sarah-Hagar cycle. Just as both Ishmael and Isaac buried Abraham earlier, now Esau and Jacob bury Isaac (v. 29). Mention of both of Isaac's sons provides a fitting conclusion to the stories of the generation of Isaac's family because it prepares the reader for the introduction to the next narrative cycle, which will begin with the genealogies of both Esau and Jacob, his two sons through his monogamous marriage to his Terahite kinswoman Rebekah.

---

ment [BWANT 130; Stuttgart: Kohlhammer, 1990]) in her study of the words *betûlâ* (virgin [according to Engelken]), *'almâ* (young woman), *pîlegeš* (secondary wife), *'āmâ* (handmaid), and *šiphâ* (maidservant). M. Bal (*Death and Dissymmetry: The Politics of Coherence in the Book of Judges* [Chicago: Univ. of Chicago Press, 1988]) argues that in Judges *pîlegeš* refers to a woman who lives with her father after she has married. Bal believes that the issue of where a woman resides after marriage is crucial in the stories in Judges. According to her, Judges is a more ancient text than Genesis; the pattern of a woman living with her father after marriage seen in Judges shifts to the situation of a wife dwelling with her husband's family as depicted in Genesis. Therefore, by the time of Genesis *pîlegeš* would have lost the meaning Bal argues for in Judges.

Chapter 4

The Rachel-Leah Cycle:
Sororal Polygyny

The lack of a stereotypical genealogical introduction to the Rachel-Leah cycle (Gen 36:1—50:26) provides the first piece of narrative evidence that this cycle ultimately does not work out themes of heirship and inheritance in the same manner as in the prior two cycles. Here genealogy does not connect directly to marriage choices, and inheritance of land does not function as an indicator of heirship decisions. If we are no longer in the sphere of working out lineal genealogies, what motivates the inclusion in Genesis of these stories about Jacob's children?

To answer that question, we can begin with the fact that Jacob's family situation differs decisively from that of both Abraham and Isaac before him. In the prior two cases, the narratives explored the manner in which the primary wife obtained a child, or children, and then addressed issues affecting the patriarch's choice of his lineal heir. By way of contrast, the stories of Jacob begin after the patriarch has already fathered twelve sons and one daughter. The Rachel-Leah cycle need not concern itself with the topic of bearing children; rather it faces the problem of deciding heirship among many children. Further, unlike the other two narrative cycles, the wives whose social status and ability to reproduce shape the course of heirship decisions never appear in these stories. At the point when the Rachel-Leah cycle begins, Rachel has already died (35:19); we only learn after the fact of Leah's death (49:31). Moreover, nothing further is heard about Zilpah after Jacob meets up with Esau (32:22) or about Bilhah after 35:22. Finally, after having already learned in Gen 35:22 that Reuben attempts to take his father's place in the Israelite lineage by acting like his father in having sexual intercourse with Bilhah, the reader expects Reuben to emerge as Jacob's lineal heir.

Hence, the Rachel-Leah cycle differs from the prior two cycles in significant details of family life, as well as in its literary genre.[1] Further—and here we begin to answer the question posed above—this cycle differs from the other two because its narrative moves from a concern with lineal/vertical heirship to a horizontal/segmented genealogy. In other words, the Rachel-Leah cycle provides us with a social model for resolving heirship in the situation of sororal polygyny. Cross-cultural kinship studies on sororal polygyny lead us to expect multiple heirship among the offspring of Rachel and Leah.[2] Sororal polygyny, then, extends heirship to multiple individuals.

Notwithstanding this arrangement for multiple heirship, social reality does not always conform to social norms. Individuals can attempt to manipulate these norms to their personal advantage.[3] The difference between the prior model of single heirship, which keeps the inheritance intact, and the present expectation of multiple heirship, which reduces the amount of inheritance available to any one heir, is the focal point of the final narrative cycle in Genesis. Tension between single and multiple heirship results because division of inheritance yields smaller shares of property (both movable and immovable goods), leading to reduced eco-

---

1. G. W. Coats (*Genesis with an Introduction to Narrative Literature* [Forms of the Old Testament Literature 1; Grand Rapids, Mich.: Eerdmans, 1983] 260) argues that "the Joseph story" is a novella.

2. J. Goody, *The Orient, the Ancient and the Primitive: Systems of Marriage and the Family in the Pre-industrial Societies of Eurasia* (Cambridge: Cambridge Univ. Press, 1990) 141.

3. See chapter 1, above, on the distinction between ideal social practice and the reality of implementing such practice; see R. Firth, "Some Principles of Social Organization," *Essays in Social Organization and Values* (London School of Economics Monographs on Social Anthropology 28; London: Athlone, 1964). For further discussion of this issue, see J. Goody, *Production and Reproduction* (Cambridge Studies in Social Anthropology 17; Cambridge: Cambridge Univ. Press, 1976) 97–98. Numerous variables, including personal greed, can intervene to separate the ideal from the reality of determining heirship.

nomic productivity for each heir. Multiple heirship comes at the expense of individual gain. Consequently, an individual might attempt to go against social norms and obtain the entire inheritance for himself.

Because the Rachel-Leah cycle focuses on a variety of subjects besides the family of Jacob, I will eschew the detailed commentary on individual pericopes provided in the past chapters. Instead, I will examine only selected incidents that bear on how the narratives relate to our larger concern with issues of family production and reproduction in Genesis.

Genesis 36:1-43

As we might expect from our examination of the previous two Genesis narrative cycles, the final one begins with a genealogical prologue written in stereotypical language. The genealogy of Esau, the son of Isaac who is not chosen to be his father's lineal heir, displays familial stability. Esau's descent line moves from one generation to the next with the same uninterrupted succession already observed in the prior genealogies of Shem (Gen 11:10-26) and Ishmael (Gen 25:12-18), two other men located outside the Terahite lineage. Generational continuity characterizes the ideal stable family situation of Esau's heirs as the lineage moves from one generation to the next.

Family history (36:1-43) is conveyed through the juxtaposition of a number of genealogical units that connect successive generations.[4] The genealogy of Esau traces the social structure of his descendants back to wives and land. For example, Gen 36:1-5 records the names of the sons born to Esau in the land of Canaan. Here we observe the formation of the genealogy of Esau through the women who became his wives. These women's names remind the reader that the Canaanite background of Esau's wives (they are Hittite, Hivite, and Ishmaelite) prevented him from be-

---

4. On this composite genealogy, see R. R. Wilson, *Genealogy and History in the Biblical World* (New Haven and London: Yale Univ. Press, 1977) 167–83. Wilson notes the same pattern discerned here, that is, genealogies as bridges between narrative units (182). He also observes that the information in 26:34 and 28:8 conflicts with what is preserved in Genesis 36. The accuracy of this information has little relevance for the present structural argument.

ing his father Isaac's lineal heir. These are the women who, from the Israelite perspective, prevented Esau from continuing Isaac's line.[5]

In vv. 6-8, the narrator breaks in to explain why Esau was forced to part company with Jacob and to remove himself and his family to Seir: the land could not accommodate both families at the same time due to their sizes. Limited resources—rather than family quarrels—result in family fission. The situation is reminiscent of the earlier separation of Abram from Lot (Genesis 13). In the last chapter we observed that Jacob and Laban also separated due to property issues; they could not live together due to their rivalry over movable goods (Genesis 31). By contrast, when Jacob and Hamor agree to live together as neighbors, Hamor convinces his people that a covenant with Jacob would be advantageous because "the land is broad enough for them" (34:21b).

Yet the matter of sufficient land to support them both appears merely to be a pretext for the real reason that the brothers Jacob and Esau separate—the matter of the inheritance of family land by Isaac's lineal heir, Jacob (v. 6b). This inheritance must not be threatened by claims from Jacob's rival heir, Esau. A situation similar to the one between Jacob and Esau occurred when Ishmael (Genesis 21) and Abraham's other sons by his concubines (Gen 25:1-6) were all sent to live away from the land that Isaac inherited from his father.

This narrative interruption (vv. 6-8) leads into the second half of Esau's genealogy, which builds on the information provided in 36:1-5. In 36:9-14 the genealogy again names Esau's wives and the sons borne to Esau by them, but now the text lists the sons fathered by Esau's sons, that is, Esau's grandchildren. This genealogical unit gives information on the branching out of Esau's lineage.

The following section, vv. 15-19, moves from the family sphere and takes on political overtones. The names from vv. 9-14 are now presented in vv. 15-19 as tribal groupings. Esau's family is now listed according to its chiefs.

The genealogy of Esau then shifts to record the first- and second-generation descendants of the Horites who dwelt in the

---

5. Further study is needed in order to understand better the social function of the placement of women's names in the Genesis 36 genealogy. The appearance of these names in this genealogy suggests the importance of women and marriage for analyzing the formation of kinship groupings.

land of Seir with Esau and his family. The genealogy of the Horites of Seir provides relatively straightforward family history—including the names of several women—and then indicates the tribal chiefs of the Horites, just as the genealogy of Esau preceding it did. One notes the name of Esau's wife, Oholibamah, among the Horite genealogical listing (36:25). The marriage between Esau and Oholibamah, exogamous by Israelite standards, appears to be one of alliance, in contrast to the Israelite marriages that are made to continue the Terahite descent line.

There is a further connection between the families of Esau and Seir recorded in this genealogy. Esau's son Eliphaz takes as a secondary wife Timna, a daughter of Seir (vv. 12, 22). Based on the information available to us in the biblical text, the latter union also appears to be an alliance marriage. Timna is related to Esau's wife Oholibamah, but Eliphaz is a son of Esau by his Hittite wife, Adah.

The genealogy then shifts from the tribal level and provides us with the names of the kings of Edom. Information on the king named last in the list, Hadar, includes not only his wife's name, but her mother's name and her grandmother's name! Kinship studies help explain the presence of multiple women's names in this lengthy genealogy: "The names of women who were taken as wives from other major descent groups are remembered in the genealogies."[6] Women's names in genealogies typically indicate that an exogamous marriage has taken place. These names make explicit that a woman has married into the patrilineage and that a marriage of alliance has been formed. Thus, the presence or absence of women's names in a genealogy typically provides data on whether a marriage establishes alliance or descent within the kinship group. This observation not only helps us to understand the inclusion of the women's names in the Esau genealogy—where marriages are exogamous—but suggests a rationale for their sup-

6. R. F. Murphy and L. Kasdan, "Agnation and Endogamy: Some Further Considerations," *Southwestern Journal of Anthropology* 23 (1967) 10. Murphy and Kasdan argue that "genealogical amnesia" regarding both men and women is a terribly complicated phenomena but that "it should never be assumed that lack of importance of ascendants is ever the cause for such absences" (11). Rather, marriage within the patrilineage allows for descent to be decided through the father, and yet it recognizes the mother; thus, the name of the mother may be omitted in order to maintain patrilineal descent (N. Jay, *Throughout Your Generations Forever: Sacrifice, Religion, and Paternity* [Chicago and London: Univ. of Chicago Press, 1992] 98–99).

pression in the patrilineal genealogy of Terah, in which case the
marriages of the primary heirs are endogamous.

Although the genealogy of 36:1-39 can easily be separated into
discrete units (vv. 1-5, 6-8, 9-14, 15-19, 20-28, 29-30, 31-39, 40-43),[7]
together these units function as a single genealogical heading to
the narratives in 37:2—50:26. The fate of the son who is no longer
eligible to be his father's Israelite heir leads into the story of the
chosen heir, in accordance with the pattern already present in the
prior two narrative cycles.

Esau's family history moves without interruption from one
generation to the next. Nothing occurs in the history of Esau's
descendants to impede the family's progression through the
generations. Esau's family genealogy provides the story of his
family's fate as the family branches out and becomes "a people,"
Edom. The genealogy emphasizes the geographical separation between Esau's descendants and those of his brother Jacob. The
separation of Israelite heir from nonlineal heir, as well as their
connection to differing lands in the Near East, repeats the kind of
information given about Ishmael and Isaac at the beginning of the
Rebekah cycle.

Genesis 37

The stories that comprise the last narrative cycle (Gen 37:2—50:26)
begin without the genealogy expected from the prior narrative
cycles (Gen 11:27-32 [Terah]; 25:19-25 [Isaac]). Instead of a problem
of heirship being introduced in the genealogy, a problem whose
resolution will come in the following narratives, we move from
a brief genealogical introduction (37:2) to the narratives of Jacob
and his sons.[8]

Despite the distinctive genealogical character of the Rachel-
Leah cycle, these stories, like the prior ones, raise many questions

---

7. The only scholarly dispute regarding this division of units is whether or
not vv. 29-30 should be separated from or included with vv. 20-28. G. von Rad
(*Genesis* [OTL; Philadelphia: Westminster, 1972] 346) connects the two units into
one. For the opposing argument, see Wilson, *Genealogy and History*, 167.

8. Genesis 37:1 appears to be a transitional verse, moving us from the genealogical superscription of Esau to the abbreviated genealogical statement
concerning Jacob; see C. Westermann, *Genesis 37–50* (Minneapolis: Augsburg,
1986) 35.

pertaining to cross-cultural kinship studies. What should a man do if he has a number of legitimate heirs?[9] Would it be more desirable to choose only one heir, even though the implications for the other eleven sons are unknown? Conversely, is the Terahite patrimony large enough that it could be shared if Jacob opted to divide his inheritance and allow the family lineage to pass through all his offspring? Might only the eight sons of Jacob's primary wives, Rachel and Leah, inherit, and the four sons of his secondary wives, Bilhah and Zilpah, not?

We gain perspective on these questions by noting the concern with family preservation and perpetuation of family that unites 37:2—50:26 with the stories that have gone before it. The Rachel-Leah cycle begins with the family of Jacob and his sons, only then to decentralize its focus on a particular heir, and ultimately to negate the search for a single heir altogether. All the while, the narrative notes that the twelve sons all belong to Jacob, and indicates who their mothers are.

The mention of Joseph (37:2a) suggests that Reuben may not function as lineal heir (35:22). This initial reference to Joseph also suggests that Simeon and Levi are no longer rivals for the position of chosen heir due to the ruse perpetrated against the Shechemites and its consequences (34:13-31). As was suggested earlier, a degree of ambiguity surrounds the motives and actions of these two brothers of Dinah. The pattern of preferred marriages emerging from the present study indicates that Simeon and Levi understand better than their father the appropriate boundaries for making marriages within the family of Terah.

If custom mandates that birth order is the sole determinant of inheritance decisions in the situation of a single heir, we would expect Reuben, Simeon, and Levi, in that order, to be heir to Jacob.[10]

---

9. From the evidence of both genealogy and narrative, Wilson (*Genealogy and History*) argues that "the assigning of the sons to different mothers implies that the sons are not related to each other as equals but are on different status levels" (185). He bases his interpretation on the fact that Jacob favors Rachel over Leah. According to Wilson, Rachel's sons have higher status than Leah's sons, while the sons of Bilhah and Zilpah have even lower status than Leah's children because their mothers are servants (185–86). From the perspective of the final form of the biblical text, I do not believe that the evidence supports Wilson's conclusions.

10. Commentators disagree on the order of heirship among Jacob's sons—assuming that a single heir is to be chosen. R. Westbrook believes that the sons should be ranked according to the statuses of their mothers, leading to Joseph be-

These three brothers are Leah's sons. Moreover, her fourth born son, Judah, provides the focus of Genesis 38—though in Genesis 37 Judah acts in a questionable manner.

The organization of the biblical material suggests that one of the functions of these narratives is to create negative impressions about Leah's first four sons. Simeon and Levi kill the Shechemites (Genesis 34); Reuben has sexual intercourse with his father's secondary wife, Bilhah (Gen 35:22); Judah withholds his son Shelah from Tamar, his daughter-in-law (Genesis 38). In narrative fashion, the redactor has eliminated these four sons as potential heirs. Hence, Joseph, a son born to Rachel after all of Leah's children have been born, acquires status as potential primary heir.

Of course, Leah's two remaining sons, Issachar and Zebulun, should also be considered as potential heirs. Yet the narrative exploration of heirship neglects them. Possibly there are negative connotations to the births of these two sons, coming as they do after conflict between Rachel and Leah results in Rachel receiving mandrakes in exchange for allowing Leah to spend the night with Jacob (30:14-20). In any case, a two-tier structure of Leah's sons emerges: four who are cast in a negative light, and two who are never explicitly considered as lineal heirs.[11]

Mention of the sons of Jacob's secondary wives, Bilhah and Zilpah (37:2c), suggests that one of these individuals could receive consideration as heir to Jacob.[12] These four sons—Dan, Naphtali, Gad, and Asher—follow next in order of birth after the four sons of Leah listed above. These sons are Joseph's brothers, and therefore, at least theoretically, rivals for the position of heir to Jacob.

---

ing next in line after Reuben (each being a firstborn son of one of Jacob's primary wives—that is, Leah and Rachel). According to Westbrook, when Ephraim and Manasseh are included in Jacob's inheritance, they are given the equivalent of the double share of the firstborn, thereby proving Joseph's position as chosen heir (*Property and the Family in Biblical Law* [JSOTSup 113; Sheffield: JSOT Press, 1991] 136). In contrast, T. Prewitt (*The Elusive Covenant* [Bloomington and Indianapolis: Indiana Univ. Press, 1990] 44–49) recognizes ambiguity in the text and presents multiple possibilities for interpreting the birth order of the sons when questions of heirship arise. As I will show, these arguments are moot because ultimately all twelve sons are included as heirs to the patrilineage of Terah through Jacob.

11. The two tiers of Leah's sons were called to my attention by Thomas B. Dozeman.

12. At this time, Bilhah and Zilpah are referred to as *nēšê*, the term used for primary wives; see Gen 16:1, where the same word is used (in the singular) to refer to Sarai, primary wife of Abram. Moreover, in Gen 16:3 Hagar is given to Abram as an *'iššâ*.

Kinship studies emphasize rivalry or jealousy over heirship as a dynamic influencing family fission, while from a literary perspective the topic of jealousy in Genesis 37 derives from the hatred all of Joseph's brothers feel toward him. The ill-will between Joseph and the sons of Bilhah and Zilpah derives partly from the fact that Joseph discredits them to his father with a bad report (37:2). The text never reveals what, if anything, serves as the basis for this information. Joseph's reports function to remove them as rivals for heirship from Jacob. Although we are not told how Jacob reacted to this information, or whether Joseph was successful in his attempt, the implication seems to be that these sons are diminished in their father's eyes. This conclusion is suggested when the text moves directly from a statement of Joseph's action to a statement of the favoritism Jacob felt toward Joseph and of the special piece of clothing that symbolized this favoritism (v. 3).

The narrative tells us that Jacob's special love for Joseph stems from the fact that "he was the son of his old age" (v. 3). For the time being, it seems that the story line will follow events in the life of Joseph, in anticipation of him becoming the next man to take his place in the vertical lineage traced back to Terah. Based on narrative precedent, but not social convention in the case of sororal polygyny, only one son from each generation could assume the status of Israelite lineal heir and claim both the family name and the land that goes with it.

In the prior narrative cycles, only one rival opposed the chosen heir, but in the case of the Rachel-Leah cycle, eleven other sons are eligible for the status of chosen heir.[13] Family fission, indeed family breakdown, comes early in the story of Jacob's family when the eleven brothers who stand to be disinherited if only one son becomes lineal heir decide to take action against the favored son, Joseph.[14] Based on their father's favoritism, the brothers fear that Jacob may designate Joseph as his lineal heir and that they will be disinherited as a result of this choice.[15] It is no wonder, then,

---

13. However, after Joseph has become the favored son, it appears that his real rival is Benjamin—the other son of Jacob's old age.

14. Cf. Coats, Genesis, 266: "The plot develops around a family crisis. By interaction between an impetuous Joseph and treacherous brothers, the family breaks apart."

15. Interest in family wealth, and family livelihood, such as we saw in the story of Laban and his sons, continues in this narrative cycle. The story emphasizes the

that Joseph's brothers hate him and are unable to speak to him in
a civilized manner (v. 4).

The sheer number of individuals who stand to be disinherited should Joseph become lineal heir increases the force of the
brothers' resolve to rid the family of the potential chosen heir and
thereby reverse their fate. Thus, while the narrative cycle begins
with an emphasis on the family, this emphasis is soon negated.[16]
From a social-scientific perspective, the family unit breaks down
when the brothers sell Joseph into slavery. From a literary perspective, the important events are that the brothers leave Joseph
to die in the wilderness (vv. 23-24), but later sell him to a caravan
of Ishmaelites/Midianites (vv. 25-28).[17] Not only are the brothers
rid of Joseph, but they have benefited financially from their transaction with the Midianites. The brothers fetch a sum of twenty
pieces of silver for Joseph (v. 28).[18]

The family—that is, the brothers interested in removing the
favored son, the likely heir—all have a hand in selling Joseph, and
they sell him to the descendants of another man who desired to be
his father's heir. All those who either have been excluded or fear
being excluded from the family inheritance are brought into the
story in a negative light, in the sense that they want to get rid of
the brother who appears destined to be heir.

---

family's flocks, part of their movable inheritance, when Joseph joins his brothers
who are out tending Jacob's sheep (37:12).

16. In theory, the choice of any of the twelve brothers as lineal heir could
generate hatred in the other eleven. The only "natural" choice, Reuben, might
not create hatred, but even in this situation the brothers could decide to challenge
the decision to designate a single heir from among them.

17. There is disagreement about the unity of this text. Despite the shift in
plan on how to get rid of Joseph, and the change from Ishmaelite to Midianite
traders, one scholar argues, "37:5-36 is basically a unit, not to be divided into
two parallel literary sources or even two widely separated editions of the same
scene" (Coats, *Genesis*, 271). Westermann maintains that more than one variant
of the story lies behind the present text (*Genesis 37-50*, 40–44). The presence of
the Ishmaelites in the story deserves mention. The descendants of the son of
Abraham who are excluded from the lineage of Terah are brought back into the
narrative, suggesting that the Genesis family stories have now come full circle.
The Ishmaelites, offspring of one son removed from the inheritance, are involved
in the scheme that ultimately removes the children of the chosen heir from this
inheritance.

18. See Gen 20:16. Abimelech pays one thousand pieces of silver to vindicate
Sarah's honor. In Genesis 24, Abraham pays four hundred pieces of silver to the
Hittites for the cave of Machpelah. On how to evaluate these sums of money, see
chapter 1 n. 38, above.

Although the three eldest sons of Leah all appear to have been eliminated as contenders for the role of Jacob's primary heir even before the Rachel-Leah cycle begins, they appear in the story either when the brothers decide to be rid of Joseph or, later, when the brothers meet Joseph and he demands that Benjamin come to Egypt. This reintroduction of characters whom we might have thought were no longer of interest to the story results in a final narrative curtain call in Genesis. In this regard, we note that in the narrative the Ishmaelites (37:25, 28) of the Sarah-Hagar cycle return, as does the burial cave that Abraham purchased. And at the conclusion of Genesis (49:29-32), we learn that all the men of the Israelite lineage beginning with Abraham and their primary wives—excluding Rachel—are buried in this spot. This information ties the narrative cycles together, as well as establishes the flow of generations in the lineage begun by Terah.

At this point in the story, the working out of the favored son's fate changes locale, providing us with a literary foreshadowing of the move from Canaan to Egypt by Jacob's family. Of course, while in Egypt, away from the land of his father, Joseph does not seem to be in a favorable position to take his place as his father's lineal heir, or even to be one of a number of multiple heirs. Ultimately the story chronicles the movement of various potential heirs back and forth between Canaan and Egypt, shifting the emphasis of the narrative from the theme of heirship to residence on the land.

After Joseph is lost to his family, several of his brothers appear in prominent roles, again with the result that the text explores the topic of potential heir to Jacob's lineage. Reuben's attempt to intervene and save Joseph from his brother's hands, and his later distress upon learning of Joseph's disappearance from the pit, would seem to be based on the prerogatives of the eldest son in assuming responsibility toward siblings and parent. I have already argued that Reuben was acting as heir apparent when he had sexual intercourse with Bilhah. The same desire to be his father's heir may explain why, in the present episode, Reuben feels Jacob will hold him accountable for the disappearance of Joseph. Reuben worries that if he cannot take responsibility to guarantee the safety of family members, he may not be designated as his father's heir.

Another potential heir, Judah, comes to the forefront of the story when he encourages the brothers to sell Joseph to the Ishmaelites instead of killing him. While Judah agrees with Reuben's intention to avoid responsibility for murder, Judah concurs with the rest of the brothers that the family should be rid of Joseph. The mere mention of Judah in this first event involving him since he was born in Gen 29:35 reminds the reader of his existence and the possibility that he too could be Jacob's lineal heir.

The story of Judah and Tamar comes as an interruption in the lives of Jacob and his sons.[19] The story formulates the question of the continuation of lineage from several different perspectives. Judah's behavior toward his sons and Tamar in particular, and women in general, may be an attempt by the narrator to suggest that Judah will be lineal heir to Jacob. In other words, prior interest in Reuben, and then Joseph, may have been false clues in discovering who the next heir will be.[20] After all, earlier, despite Isaac's favoritism toward Esau, Rebekah's favorite son, Jacob, ultimately became Isaac's Israelite heir. The same may now be true in the case of Jacob's favoritism toward Joseph. Thus, Judah could be heir apparent to Jacob.

Genesis 38

Genesis 38 concerns family continuity through the line of Judah. We are informed of Judah's marriage to a Canaanite woman, of the three sons she bore him, and then of the chain of events that occur when the firstborn son, Er, marries a woman named Tamar, whom Judah finds for him. Although the Canaanite background of Judah's wife is made explicit, Tamar's lineage is never mentioned. Does this silence warrant our assumption that Tamar is a "proper" wife for Er? Is there no longer an interest in the family background of the bride? Or does the Canaanite heritage of Judah's wife automatically eliminate him as the possible lineal heir to Jacob, as earlier Esau's Canaanite wives eliminated him?

The early death of Er occasions Judah to pass Tamar to Onan as a wife, in accordance with the principle of levirate marriage.[21]

---

19. Most commentators consider this chapter "an intrusion." See, for example, B. Vawter, *On Genesis: A New Reading* (Garden City, N.Y.: Doubleday, 1977) 389.

20. L. H. Silberman speaks of "how a false lead is constructed" in the stories of Jacob's sons ("Listening to the Text," *JBL* 102 [1983] 23).

21. Many others have observed that the biblical narratives do not strictly follow

The marriage between a woman and her brother-in-law, in the circumstance that no male child already exists to transmit the name and property of the dead husband/brother,[22] becomes an heirship strategy designed to carry on the line of the husband/brother, but it also provides the widow with the right to a son who will provide her with protection in her old age.[23] This story allows us to glimpse new strategies of heirship. The birth of this child not only perpetuates the lineage of his dead father; it also establishes the lineal heir for his grandfather, in this case Judah.

The story thus far continues to exhibit interest in the primary topics uniting the ancestral narratives, heirship and inheritance. Furthermore, the transfer of a widow of a dead brother to a living one is a recognized heirship strategy in patrilineal societies such as ancient Israel.[24]

News of Tamar's pregnancy brings the wrath of Judah, who demands her death for having violated his family's honor. When Tamar refutes his charges of prostitution by demonstrating that Judah fathered her child,[25] her father-in-law acknowledges that she has assumed a greater responsibility for guaranteeing the continuity of family than he himself has done. He may also be recognizing the rights of his widowed daughter-in-law to a child.[26]

---

the law of the levirate as specified in Deut 25:5-10. Westbrook concludes that the law applies only when property is involved and the inheritance has not yet been divided. For his general discussion of the levirate laws in the Hebrew Bible, see *Property and the Family*, 69–89. For the argument that Onan's actions in Genesis 38 should be interpreted as his attempt to obtain the firstborn's share of a double inheritance, see H. C. Brichto, "Kin, Cult, Land and Afterlife—A Biblical Complex," *HUCA* 44 (1973) 16; and T. Thompson and D. Thompson, "Some Legal Problems in the Book of Ruth," *VT* 18 (1968) 93–94.

22. Westbrook (*Property and the Family*, 76) notes, "Only in Genesis is no specific reference to the inheritance made. The first step alone is mentioned, that of raising up seed for the deceased."

23. G. W. Coats, "Widow's Rights: A Crux in the Structure of Gn 38," *CBQ* 34 (1972) 461–66.

24. For cross-cultural data on the levirate, see Goody, *Production and Reproduction*.

25. One notes how quickly Judah accepts responsibility for what has happened. He could have denied that the items were his, or at the very least accused Tamar of becoming pregnant by another man—despite his having had sexual intercourse with her. After all, there were no biological tests to determine paternity. Or, is it a source of male pride to have impregnated a woman?

26. On how a widow's rights to a child also guarantee her a place in the inheritance of her deceased husband, consult Thompson and Thompson, "Some Legal Problems," 79–99.

How the narrator evaluates Judah's actions is initially difficult to determine. Should judgment be passed on him, first, for marrying a Canaanite wife, and, second, for withholding Shelah from Tamar, and then for having sexual intercourse with his daughter-in-law? Or should all be forgiven because Judah's lineage lives on, notwithstanding the fact that Judah, like Lot (Gen 19:30-38), was an unknowing participant in the continuation of his lineage?[27] It may well be that as in the case of Lot's daughters, Judah's ultimate aim is to perpetuate the family line no matter what else may happen. In the end, however, the story about Judah appears to be yet another misleading attempt to designate Jacob's lineal heir.[28]

Genesis 39–41

The story of Joseph's encounter with Potiphar's wife again brings up the topic of the correct woman for an Israelite man. Potiphar's wife does not fall within the preferred group of spouses for Joseph, the more so because she is already married. Under these circumstances, Joseph has no right to any claim on this woman. An adulterous relationship does not legitimize a man as heir to the lineage through Terah. Joseph realizes this. He does nothing to violate social norms, but whether he will finally marry within the prescribed kinship boundaries remains to be resolved. Even if a married Israelite woman had attempted to seduce Joseph, his action still would have been wholly inappropriate. Thus, the text comments on marriage between an Israelite man and a married woman, regardless of her lineage.

---

27. The chiastic structure that Prewitt finds behind the Genesis narratives locates Genesis 38 in a position corresponding to Genesis 19 (*Elusive Covenant*, 80). Westbrook distinguishes between incest and the levirate responsibility in these texts (*Property and the Family*, 85–87).

28. Contra Silberman ("Listening to the Text," 23–24) and Prewitt ("Kinship Structures and the Genesis Genealogies," *JNES* 40 [1981] 97–98), the conclusion that Judah is the chosen heir is only defensible if one reads the biblical text from hindsight, and fits it primarily within the time frame of the monarchy. The emphasis on Judah as heir makes less sense if one argues for the formation of these texts in the exilic or postexilic period. Furthermore, the argument that the text establishes Judah as heir depends on the information in Gen 48:8-12. No other text in the Rachel-Leah cycle supports such a conclusion.

In earlier chapters, I have shown that in other narrative cycles in Genesis, women play important roles in legitimizing men as heirs to the Terahite lineage; in this narrative cycle, women play a less important role in that regard. Women appear infrequently in these stories, and when they do, the subject of appropriate marriage is seldom broached.[29] Besides the marriage of Judah to a Canaanite woman, and his subsequent sexual encounter with his daughter-in-law Tamar, the only other marriage occurring in the story takes place between Joseph and Asenath, the daughter of an Egyptian priest (41:45; 46:20). Joseph ultimately marries outside the boundaries for an "appropriate" wife. The marriage union produces two sons, Ephraim and Manasseh, whom Jacob, before his death, includes as full heirs to his inheritance (48:5). These grandsons are now of equivalent heirship status to biological sons of Jacob. Any potential problem that Joseph's marriage to a woman outside the Terahite lineage may have presented to his father's kinship group is resolved when Jacob gives inheritance rights to Manasseh and Ephraim.[30]

Genesis 42–50

The resolution of the tensions dividing Jacob's family against itself highlights the sons we have already discussed as heirs to the family name and fortune. Genesis 42 reminds us of Reuben's plan in chapter 37 to intervene on behalf of Joseph. Now Reuben works on behalf of Benjamin, the remaining son of Jacob's old age. Reuben goes so far as to guarantee his own sons as collateral for Benjamin when Jacob refuses to allow him to be brought to Egypt (42:37). Reuben endangers his own lineage in order to appease his father.

---

29. Consult Prewitt (*Elusive Covenant*) for his structural understanding of the marriages and relationships between men and women in the latter part of Genesis.

30. Westbrook asserts that this is not a case of adoption (*Property and the Family*, 136 n. 2). Jay notes that Jacob considers Ephraim and Manasseh to be like Reuben and Simeon (48:5), that is, sons of Leah, rather than sons of Rachel like their father Joseph, because Rachel's theft of the teraphim threatened descent through the father. She argues that any future children born to Joseph could not be recognized as heirs to Jacob, but she relates this to the teraphim incident rather than to Joseph's Egyptian wife Asenath (*Throughout Your Generations*, 109).

As Reuben did earlier, Judah too reenters the story and takes responsibility for the fate of Benjamin in Egypt (43:8-9). On the one hand, the text highlights Reuben and Judah and their attempts to preserve the family and their father. On the other hand, the emphasis on Jacob's concern for Benjamin's safety and eventual return to his father suggests that Rachel's younger son may in fact be the next heir to the Terahite patrilineage.[31]

It appears that while family fission characterizes the earlier part of the Rachel-Leah cycle, individual brother's actions work toward family fusion as the narrative winds toward its conclusion. Family fusion occurs when Joseph arranges for Jacob and his sons to journey to him in Egypt. Chapter 46 stresses the preservation of the *entire* family of Jacob[32] in its list of family units according to the four wives of the patriarch. The list is striking for the emphasis it places on Leah, Rachel, Zilpah, and Bilhah as both wives of Jacob and mothers of his children. All of Jacob's wives' sons are counted as his direct descendants. When the family moves down to Egypt, the emphasis on family fusion stems not from property and inheritance decisions but from concern with social survival as a distinct unit in a new land. Without land as an indicator of descent from the Terahite lineage, the sons' direct descendancy from Jacob legitimates them as members of this lineage.[33]

The marriage arrangement of sororal polygyny results in an alternative to selecting only one son as his father's primary heir. The boundaries for heirship expand in this narrative cycle. Sororal polygyny leads to multiple heirship, as is evident in the story of Jacob offering blessing to Joseph's sons (Genesis 48).[34] The result of this blessing is that Jacob's half-Egyptian grandsons are

---

31. Thus, should a single heir be chosen by Jacob, it would seem that a combination of factors determines this choice. See the discussion in n. 10, above.

32. Before the family arrives in Egypt, Yahweh promises Jacob that one day they will return to the land of their inheritance. Furthermore, the patriarch is told that his family will become a great nation while they are in exile (42:3-4).

33. For further discussion of this topic, see chapter 5, below. My argument here resembles that of D. L. Smith, who writes of the exilic community: "On the basis of our analogies from sociological investigation, we might suspect that the relations with outsiders intensified the familial bonds" (D. L. Smith, *The Religion of the Landless* [Bloomington, Ind.: Meyer-Stone, 1989] 116).

34. Commentators are puzzled by Jacob's reference to Rachel's death as he prepares to include Ephraim and Manasseh as his heirs. E. A. Speiser explains, "Death had robbed Jacob of his beloved Rachel.... Hence Jacob feels justified in substituting two of Rachel's grandsons for such other sons as fate may have

made heirs along with his own sons, and they are all included in the patriarchal inheritance. Verse 4 helps us to understand the connection between this blessing and future inheritance of the father's land. The earlier message of the Sarah-Hagar and Rebekah cycles that birth order provides no guarantee in the resolution of heirship is repeated when Jacob crosses his hands and gives priority to Joseph's younger son Ephraim, instead of the elder son, Manasseh (v. 14).

The lack of interest in exclusivity of heirship also becomes clear when Jacob blesses his twelve sons in Genesis 49. The blessing includes all these sons as the future tribes of Israel. The shift from family level to national level notwithstanding, no one son is singled out as lineal heir to Jacob. Instead, the lineage clearly shifts from vertical to horizontal reckoning. Heirship has become decentralized.

Once it is absolutely clear that the pattern of designating a lineal heir to the descent group of Terah breaks down in these narratives, Jacob dies to the story and the Rachel-Leah cycle quickly draws to a close. We remember the prior connection between patrilineage and land inheritance when Jacob's sons temporarily depart Egypt to bury their father in the cave of Machpelah, which Abraham bought as a burial spot (50:13). Earlier Jacob specifically requested that he be buried in this cave along with the other members of the Terahite patrilineage: Abraham, Sarah, Isaac, Rebekah, and Leah (49:31). All those of the generations when the lineage was determined vertically and heirship included land and descent lie together in the original family burial plot, along with Jacob and Leah.

The death and delayed burial of Joseph (50:24-26) point toward the future and the change from exclusivity to inclusivity of heirship. Now that all twelve sons are designated as the horizontal descent line, the family dwells away from the land of the fathers, and Joseph's body must remain in Egypt until the family again takes possession of the patrimony. When brothers dwell together on the ancestral land, family fission results; life removed from this land brings about family fusion. The former living condition tears the Terahite patrilineage apart, while the latter condition brings it together.

---

prevented her from bearing" (*Genesis* [AB; Garden City, N.J.: Doubleday, 1964] 359).

The Question of Secondary Wives

A question referred to earlier remains before us: Why are the sons of Bilhah and Zilpah included as chosen heirs when earlier Hagar's son Ishmael could not be so included? Why do secondary wives' sons inherit in one generation when they did not inherit in an earlier generation? The difference in resolution of heirship claims may simply be a function of the number of sons of secondary wives competing for a place in the lineage, as opposed to the lone voice of Ishmael. The pattern may shift as long as there is flexibility in social organization and in the decision-making process on social organization. Kinship decisions reflect the demands of those who participate in them. In the Rachel-Leah cycle, strategies of heirship may be more loosely defined due to the number of competing claims of Jacob's sons by his two primary and two secondary wives. The result is that the rules for resolving heirship change in this final narrative cycle.

Another possibility does suggest itself, however. While Sarah, Rachel, and Leah all indicate that they will obtain children for themselves through their maids, only the sisters Rachel and Leah name the sons borne for them by secondary wives. When Ishmael is born, neither Sarah nor Hagar names him, Abram does. And that occurs despite the instruction from the angel of Yahweh that Hagar will call the child's name Ishmael (16:11). By contrast, when the secondary wives Bilhah and Zilpah bear children, the primary wives Rachel and Leah name them. The bond between the children of the secondary wives and the primary wives may be of a different quality than in the earlier narrative, thereby strengthening the claims to heirship of these four sons.[35] The end result is that four sons borne by Bilhah and Zilpah are included as Jacob's heirs because the text never excludes them.

Because no son is excluded, all the sons are heirs. By default, the patrilineage of Terah shifts from vertical to horizontal listing in the generation of the sons of Jacob. From a literary perspective, the story loses interest in choosing a lineal heir. Moreover, from an anthropological perspective, we may understand this shift by noting that the combination of vertical and horizontal genealogies

---

35. Prewitt refers to this act of naming as "signs of their legal acceptance" (*Elusive Covenant*, 44).

results in the structural creation of "a true family tree."[36] The shift from a unilineal to a segmented genealogy yields "genealogical depth"; it allows us to trace multiple descent lines for the Terahite patrilineage.

Comparison with the Earlier Cycles

We have seen in this chapter that the Rachel-Leah cycle shares an interest in the topics of lineage and heirship characteristic of the prior narratives and yet that these issues are never resolved in the generation of Jacob's twelve sons. In the earlier two narrative cycles, we learned that the son chosen as heir must reside on the land he inherits. But all of Jacob's sons leave Canaan and dwell in Egypt. None of them meets the residency requirement observed for heirship in the other family stories of Genesis.

My discussion of the function of land and its connection to genealogy in the prior narrative cycles suggests that the texts of Gen 36:1—50:26 both complement and provide commentary on the earlier ones when we examine the pattern that emerges for determining heirship. As I have already remarked, the final narrative cycle has less interest in whether or not Jacob's sons enter into "appropriate" marriages. Furthermore, it is not consistent with the prior two cycles on the resolution of heirship and inheritance. Typically, descent groups are concerned with the transfer of property—especially land—from one generation to the next, as was the case in the Sarah-Hagar and the Rebekah cycles. However, the message of the Rachel-Leah cycle seems to be that lineage boundaries should not be so tightly drawn as in prior generations. The text connects the widening of kinship boundaries with the loss of land. When brothers attempt to dwell together and share the land, family conflict results. Hence, the son of Hagar does not inherit as Abraham's heir, but the sons of Jacob's secondary wives, Bilhah and Zilpah, do.

What distinguishes the fate of this generation of sons from the prior two concerns not only the marriage arrangements of their

---

36. A. Malamat, "Tribal Societies: Biblical Genealogies and African Lineage Systems," *Archives européennes de sociologie* 14 (1973) 127. I am grateful to Malamat for calling my attention to this study and for providing me with a copy of his article.

parents but the important matter of the connection between heirship and remaining in the land.[37] Earlier we learned that Isaac
must remain in the land of his father's sojournings at all costs in
order to be Abraham's heir, while Jacob's return from his time in
Paddan-aram with Laban becomes the occasion for designating
him as Isaac's heir. The connection between Israelite patrilineage
and continuous dwelling in the land is made patently clear in
the latter case: "And Jacob came to his father Isaac at Mamre,
or Kiriath-arba (that is, Hebron), where Abraham and Isaac had
sojourned" (35:27).

This narrative cycle explains how the family of Jacob came to
live outside the land of the sojournings of Abraham and Isaac, the
patrimony of the Terahite lineage. At the same time, it makes explicit that the sons of Jacob are all properly descended from this
patrilineage. These offspring are all branches of Terah's descent
line. The marriages of Jacob and Rachel and Leah provide the justification for a shift from a vertical to a horizontal genealogy. This
shift occurs because the sisters Rachel and Leah are equal in status
as primary wives of Jacob, and the sons of the secondary wives,
Bilhah and Zilpah, are included as heirs to their father.

---

37. See D. Steinmetz (*From Father to Son* [Louisville: Westminster/John Knox
Press, 1991] 152–53), who reaches similar conclusions, though from a different
methodological perspective.

Chapter 5

Conclusions

The present disarray in pentateuchal studies is symptomatic of an upheaval in Hebrew Bible scholarship. While reexamining the results of earlier research, scholars search for alternative methodological models. Social-scientific methods provide one such new perspective. Biblical scholars use social-scientific analysis to reconstruct the social world behind the text. As part of this effort, the present study attempts to demonstrate the relevance of anthropological insights for interpreting the Hebrew Bible by examining the ancestral stories of Genesis in light of cross-cultural kinship data. In particular, this investigation of Gen 11:10—50:26 demonstrates that the subjects of heirship, marriage, and ownership of land in the ancestral stories are of paramount importance as one seeks to understand this literature.

Narrative Criticism
within a Genealogical Framework

This study interprets the biblical text through a method that connects narratives to the relevant genealogies. When narrative is read within a genealogical framework, a pattern emerges that makes it possible to identify Gen 11:10 as the dividing point separating the end of primeval history from the beginning of Israelite history. Moreover, this approach allows us to analyze the

135

literary functions of both genealogy and narrative in the Genesis ancestral stories: narrative and genealogy make up stories. Interrelated narrative episodes establish the criteria for determining heirship in each generation of ancestors, while genealogies provide the links between generations. Genealogy also represents the uninterrupted movement from one generation to the next. When problems occur that threaten the continuation of genealogy, narratives interrupt to explore and resolve these generational issues. I have argued that one cannot fully articulate the dilemma facing each generation of ancestors without knowledge of the genealogy that introduces it. In the final formation of the text, genealogy and narrative are inextricably linked.

By attending to the interrelationship of genealogy and narrative, the reader may distinguish three narrative cycles in Genesis. Genealogy (11:10-32; 25:12-26; 36:1—37:2) gives way to the narratives of family history (12:1—25:11; 25:27—35:29; 37:3—50:26), which eventually lead back to genealogy. This structural organization may be further subdivided. All three narrative cycles begin with the uninterrupted genealogy of an individual outside the descent line of Terah, that is, a genealogical superscription or prologue. This genealogical superscription precedes the genealogy of an heir chosen to continue the Terahite patrilineage. The latter is then followed by a series of narratives that explore and designate the next heir to the patrilineage. The resolution to the problem of heirship in the next generation brings the narrative cycle to a close. This pattern then repeats itself.

Recognition of this pattern connecting genealogies to narratives yields the following outline of the ancestral stories: the genealogy of Shem (11:10-26) introduces the genealogy of Terah (11:27-32), which is followed by the stories of Terah's offspring (12:1—25:11). The genealogy of Ishmael (12:12-18) leads into the genealogy of Isaac (25:19-26), whose story continues in the subsequent narratives (25:27—35:29). Finally, the genealogy of Esau (36:1-43) precedes the abbreviated genealogy of Jacob (37:2), which introduces the stories of his sons (37:3—50:26). In each case, only after resolution of the genealogical problem and the designation of a lineal heir does narrative again give way to genealogy, and family history then moves to the next generation.

This conclusion concerning the integral interconnection between genealogy and narrative requires that we reject M. Noth's argument, which construes genealogies as secondary links between narratives. The interrelationship between genealogy and narrative allows the reader to see both structural and thematic unity on heirship and descent in the family stories of Genesis.[1]

The insights of literary criticism combined with the perspectives of social-scientific analysis provide complementary perspectives for examining family structure in Gen 11:10—50:26. Cross-cultural kinship models provide the background for interpreting the resolution of the literary predicaments encountered in the genealogies. The kinship patterns that emerge from my study are consistent with cross-cultural data on heirship and marriage. These cross-cultural kinship parallels indicate that the genealogies and narratives of Genesis reflect social structures that must have made sense to the ancient authors and readers. Anthropological data allow the researcher to interpret kinship relationships in the ancestral texts in order to reconstruct ancient Israelite social structure based on categories of kinship grounded in actual life.

Kinship Categories

Cross-cultural kinship categories help us to discover how issues of production and reproduction in the family stories unite individual narrative cycles and link these cycles to each other.[2] In particular, anthropological models of family organization emphasize the importance of the following issues in Genesis: marriage choice,

---

1. R. H. Moye ("In the Beginning: Myth and History in Genesis and Exodus," *JBL* 109 [1990] 577–98) argues that the relationship between myth and history, and the structural pattern connecting genealogy with narrative in Genesis and Exodus, reveal that "the story of the Pentateuch as a whole is preeminently the story of the fall, or the exile, of humanity from the harmony of paradise and the perfect balance and order of God's creation into the disordered realm of human history and the subsequent desire for a reunion with the divine, a reunion that is accomplished not by a return to a mythical Eden but by the manifestation of the divine on earth and within history and by the return to a human and historical version of Eden, the promised land given to the chosen people by God" (598). On the theological unity of Genesis, see T. W. Mann, "All the Families of the Earth," *Int* 45 (1991) 341–53.

2. Kinship analysis depends on the social construction of gender. For an attempt to bring these two areas of study together as one, see the essays in *Gender and Kinship* (eds. J. F. Collier and S. J. Yanagisako; Stanford, Calif.: Stanford Univ. Press, 1987). In the present study of the Genesis family stories we see the connection between gender and kinship: continued inclusion in the marriage unit depends upon one's ability to reproduce for the kinship group.

heirship decisions, and division of inheritance. The diversity of potential marriage arrangements explains how and why individuals choose their marriage partners. For example, Abraham takes a secondary wife, Hagar, when his primary wife, Sarah, appears unable to bear him an heir. The distinction between a primary and a secondary wife provides for the resolution of heirship and inheritance in the succeeding generation. After Sarah gives birth to Isaac, Hagar's son, Ishmael, no longer functions as Abraham's heir because the legal rights of a primary wife take precedence over those of a secondary wife. I have argued that Abraham takes a secondary wife, rather than divorcing his barren primary wife, due to the economic basis of the union between Abraham and Sarah.

These diverse marriage arrangements may be classified in the following ways: polycoity in Gen 11:10—25:11, monogamy in Gen 25:12—35:29, and sororal polygyny in Gen 36:1—50:26. These labels for marriage structures allow us to understand that marriage is categorized from the perspective of the husband, according to the sexual unions that connect the husband to the various women in his household. These categories for various forms of marriage make it possible to interpret Genesis with great precision since we may now recognize that differing strategies of heirship provide the rationale for diverse marriage arrangements in each of the three narrative cycles. One among several potential examples is that of Sarah and Hagar given above. In this case, the distinction between primary and secondary wives allows us to understand how heirship decisions are made in Abraham's generation. Judgments on heirship are determined on the basis of the statuses of the women in the marriage because the status of the mother in most cases determines the status of her offspring.

This study has focused on the impact of several marriage arrangements—polycoity, monogamy, and sororal polygyny—for determining heirship in each of the narrative cycles. The centrality of the women for resolving heirship decisions in the stories provides justification for naming each of the family cycles in Genesis after the women whose marriage arrangement and fertility shape the course of events in the family history: Gen 11:10—25:11, the "Sarah-Hagar cycle"; Gen 25:12—35:29, the "Rebekah cycle"; and Gen 36:1—50:26, the "Rachel-Leah cycle."

This study also has revealed that patrilineal endogamous marriages establish the patrilineage of Terah. A son becomes his father's patrilineal heir only if his mother descends from the Terahite lineage. Moreover, the son must marry a bride who is also a member of this lineage. Isaac, rather than Ishmael, becomes Abraham's primary heir not only because he has the "correct" father and mother, but also because he marries an "appropriate" wife, a woman descended through the Terahite patrilineage. Bride and groom are patrilineal collateral kin; they both trace their ancestry back to the founder of the lineage, Terah. The proper wife for the lineal heir is a woman from the collateral lineage of Terah. From the perspective of both the bride and groom, priority in establishing a primary marriage goes to an individual whose parents both descend from the Terahite lineage, that is, a patrilineal kin. This pattern for marriage formation in Genesis helps explain Abraham's statement in Gen 20:12, namely, that Sarah is indeed his sister (his kinswoman), through the descent line of his father.

The narratives of Gen 11:10—35:29 establish boundaries of exclusivity in the Terahite lineage through these endogamous marriages. A pattern emerges indicating clearly that in the ancestral stories marriage functions to establish the Terahite descent line. Cross-cultural data, which connect patrilineal endogamy with kinship groups emphasizing inheritance, corroborate this pattern.[3] Marriage to one's patrilineal kin functions to keep property within this group. This conclusion refutes the argument of those who have maintained that marriage in Genesis functions to establish alliance.

Furthermore, in the first two narrative cycles, heirship results in receiving both the patrilineal name (that is, becoming the lineal heir to the Terahite patrilineage) and the patrimony—including rights to the burial cave of Machpelah (49:31). The heir's rights to the family inheritance may be observed most clearly in Gen 25:1-6, the notice of Abraham's marriage to Keturah, as well as to other women. Abraham provides gifts for his children by these

---

3. J. Goody, *Production and Reproduction* (Cambridge Studies in Social Anthropology 17; Cambridge: Cambridge Univ. Press, 1976). Even though N. Jay's study is not concerned with the final form of the text, her comments are most appropriate: "Having taken patrilineal descent for granted, scholars cannot see its establishment as an achievement, and consequently they cannot ask how it is achieved" (*Throughout Your Generations Forever: Sacrifice, Religion, and Paternity* [Chicago and London: Univ. of Chicago Press, 1992] 110).

other women so that Isaac's inheritance as lineal heir will not be negated. Moreover, in the cases of Isaac and Jacob, the right of heirship—that is, the right to receive ownership of the land—requires that the heirs reside on the patrimony.

Attention to kinship categories indicates that the final narrative cycle in Genesis also concerns heirship. Yet fundamental differences distinguish Gen 36:1—50:26 from 11:10—35:29. First, while the Sarah-Hagar and Rebekah cycles treat the search for a vertical/lineal heir, the Rachel-Leah cycle shifts to a concern for multiple/horizontal heirship. Second, in 11:10—35:29 heirship is partially determined by choice of marriage partner, a requirement of little concern in 36:1—50:26. Finally, heirship in the former cases requires residence on the land, while in the latter example heirship comes in the context of life away from this land. This finding indicates that the final narrative cycle is informed by different cross-cultural kinship categories than the former cycles. The differences between the stories underscore the need for redaction-critical study on the relationship of the Rachel-Leah cycle to the Sarah-Hagar and Rebekah cycles that precede it.

I conclude that, in the first two cycles of stories, when heirship is lineal, inheritance typically reflects concern for both land ownership and a man's place in the vertical Terahite genealogy. By contrast, in the last narrative cycle, a shift from vertical to horizontal genealogy occurs when the family no longer dwells on the patrimonial land. Once land is no longer the focus of inheritance, all twelve sons of Jacob are included in the Terahite lineage.

The shift from vertical to horizontal genealogy in the generation of Jacob's offspring reflects Jacob's marriages to the sisters Rachel and Leah. That Rachel and Leah are both primary wives of Jacob justifies including all their sons, as well as those of their maids, Jacob's secondary wives, Bilhah and Zilpah, as heirs to Jacob.

In the case of Jacob's marriages to Rachel and Leah, sororal polygyny functions as a device to help explain the shift from vertical to horizontal genealogy. The switch to a horizontal genealogy occurs at the time of the exile of Jacob's family to Egypt. The loosening of kinship boundaries comes with the loss of land. This loss brings a move from exclusivity to inclusivity of individuals within the Terahite group. Multiple heirship through the Terahite lineage comes only at the time the heirs are removed from the family patrimony. These multiple heirs no longer receive land as part of their inheritance, but they do receive the patrilineal name.

In these changed family circumstances, membership within the community is determined through one's ability to demonstrate lineage links to the name of Terah. Furthermore, the prior narrative interest in the appropriate wife for the chosen heir no longer pervades the Rachel-Leah cycle. Although a few women appear in these final stories, with the exception of Tamar in Genesis 38, they do not fulfill important roles in the history of the family. In particular, their function in legitimating sons as heirs to the Terahite lineage is lost. We are told nothing about the lineage links of these women, with the exception of the information that Joseph's wife Asenath is an Egyptian. Even in Tamar's case, lineage remains obscure.

In the case of the generation of Jacob's sons, the narrative reaches negative results on the subject of the chosen heir.[4] Despite what at times appears to be consideration of Joseph, Judah, Simeon, Reuben, and Benjamin as heirs, the Rachel-Leah cycle includes all the brothers, and two grandsons, as Jacob's heirs. By default, all of Jacob's family become his heirs as they share the destiny of (temporary) removal from the land. The conclusion of the Genesis ancestral stories establishes that the heirs to the Terahite lineage are a family residing outside their land. The narrative expects that one day these heirs will return to their patrimony (50:24-25). Together they share this fate because they are all equal to each other and all are potential lineal heirs to their father. They share the patrilineal name—they are sons of Israel.

Land and Property

We now return to the topic of land. In the first two narrative cycles, the chosen heir receives both the family name and family land, establishing the connection between heirship and remaining in the land. In the Sarah-Hagar cycle, Abraham insists that Isaac must remain in the land if he is to become heir to the Terahite patrilineage. In the Rebekah cycle, only after Jacob returns from life in Paddanaram with Laban does he receive the designation as Isaac's heir. In the latter case, the text explicitly links Israelite patrilineage and

---

4. See chapter 4 n. 28, above.

presence in the land: "And Jacob came to his father Isaac at Mamre, or Kiriath-arba (that is, Hebron), where Abraham and Isaac had sojourned" (35:27).

However, in the final narrative cycle, the entire family moves out of the land. Here the connection between heirship and land is severed. Membership in the lineage no longer depends upon dwelling in the land of the patrilineage. The lineage of Terah now continues through a family of brothers; membership in the lineage depends upon one's ability to demonstrate genealogical connection back to the sons of Israel who left the land. Israel only becomes Israel in this generation once it dwells as a family outside the boundaries of Israel.

The Rachel-Leah cycle may be critical of the earlier cycles, which appear to indicate that, while living in the land of Israel, someone must be excluded from the patrilineage—possibly due to the limited amount of land. This conclusion is consistent with cross-cultural data that designate that only one individual may be his father's heir in order that limited patrilineal landholdings will not have to be divided up.[5] Such division would diminish the amount available to each heir and limit the productivity of the group on a small parcel of land.

In sum, the Rachel-Leah cycle explains how the family of Jacob was structured outside the land of the sojournings of Abraham and Isaac, the patrilineage of Terah. At the same time, it makes explicit that the sons of Jacob are all properly genealogically connected to the genealogy of Terah. Genesis 36–50 is linked with 12–35 both structurally and thematically. The unity and diversity connecting the final narrative cycle to the earlier two raise the question of the function of the Rachel-Leah cycle in its present context.

Anthropology and History

I return now to a topic raised in chapter 1—namely, the connection between anthropology and history. In this study I reconstruct

---

5. L. E. Stager, "The Archaeology of the Family in Ancient Israel," *BASOR* 260 (1985) 25; J. Goody, *The Orient, the Ancient and the Primitive: Systems of Marriage and the Family in the Pre-industrial Societies of Eurasia* (Cambridge: Cambridge Univ. Press, 1990).

the social world within the text without paying specific attention to the sociohistorical setting that might provide the backdrop
for these stories. Such an approach is justifiable because neither
literary criticism nor comparative kinship studies concern themselves with the dynamic of change. Cross-cultural kinship data
provide models that are applicable in diverse historical circumstances. However, despite the appropriateness of the synchronic
method for purposes of this study, I prefer to address briefly considerations of change in the Genesis ancestral stories. The element
of innovation occasioned by new sociohistorical conditions is relevant to this investigation based on the differences between the
Rachel-Leah cycle and the Sarah-Hagar and Rebekah cycles. At
this point I offer some programmatic suggestions on the congruity
of synchronic and diachronic analysis for further study of the ancestral traditions. In particular, I suggest we consider postexilic
Israel as the locus for the final redaction of these texts.

What do the stories of Israel's ancestors have in common with
sociohistorical dynamics in the postexilic period? I assert that
the stories of Genesis are a literary mechanism for establishing
identity. They are metaphors for determining the boundaries of
community. Kinship structures become metaphors for social structure. Genealogy functions to establish family membership in a *bêt
'ābôt*, the kinship group. Only those who are able to trace their genealogy back to the family of Jacob—that is, to those who were
removed from the land and were in exile—constitute the true
Israel.[6] Family, or genealogy, becomes a means to legitimate the
power structure in postexilic community organization and to give
status to the returned group. Those who have been in exile, the
sons of Israel who left the patrimonial land, are the true heirs
to the Terahite lineage; they are the ones who can trace their ge-

---

6. See n. 13, below. On the shift from *bêt 'ab* to *bêt 'ābôt*, D. L. Smith remarks:
"What we must refer to is a unique post-exilic construct, called a *Bēt 'Ābôt*,
similar in *numbers* to the pre-exilic *Mišpĕḥôt*, but in nomenclature and solidarity
more similar to the pre-exilic *Bēt 'Āb*, from which the name obviously comes,
suggesting a 'collective' of *Bēt 'Āb*s" (*The Religion of the Landless* [Bloomington,
Ind.: Meyer-Stone, 1989] 102). Jay comments: "After the Exile, issues of descent
had a unique urgency, for there was an immediate problem of deciding who
among the returning exiles was a descendant of Abraham with rights in the
community. It is typical that the priesthood clung to patrilineal descent as the
only way to legitimate this inheritance. Ezra 2:59-63 refers to this time: 'Those
who could not prove their father's house or their descent...were excluded from
the priesthood as unclean'" (*Throughout Your Generations*, 96–97).

nealogy back to the patrilineal name Israel. They are entitled to membership in the restored community.

This suggestion, however tentative, accords well with data on the social function of origin traditions. Such traditions are anachronistic in that they are the most recent to take shape, though they may be based in prior tradition, and are intended to legitimize conditions at the time they are committed to writing.[7] We are dealing with stories intended to rationalize a particular social reality. In this case, Genesis legitimizes community boundaries in postexilic Israel not only through its interest in proper genealogical credentials, but also with its emphasis on entering into an "appropriate" marriage while dwelling in the land of the Terahite lineage (Genesis 12–36). That foreign wives are "inappropriate" spouses is an idea expressed in postexilic Israel. Ezra 9 addresses the problem of maintaining exclusivity within the community after so many Israelite men have married non-Israelite women while living in exile. Ezra 10 stresses that such marriages to foreign women must be terminated; vv. 18–44 list the names of the men who divorced themselves from their foreign wives. This postexilic concern with proper genealogical connections after a family has been removed from its land (Genesis 36–50) suggests that while in exile, people could marry whomever they wanted, since Joseph did. The prior narrative interest in "appropriate" wives as being important while living in the land is demonstrated when the lineage is kept pure through marriage to "correct" women (Genesis 12–35). The emphasis on the necessity of "appropriate" women as

---

7. Concerning origin traditions, see K. W. Whitelam, "Israel's Traditions of Origin: Reclaiming the Land," *JSOT* 44 (1989) 19–42. Whitelam remarks, "As we have seen, traditions of origin cannot be accepted uncritically as accurate historical records but rather very often reflect the self-perceptions of later groups projected back into history in order to legitimize their claims to rule or occupy territory.... Even if such origin traditions are late constructions, they remain valuable sources for the historian, not as witnesses to the earlier period they purport to describe, but rather to the later sociopolitical processes that shaped and adapted them" (31). See also D. J. A. Clines, *The Theme of the Pentateuch* (JSOTSup 10; Sheffield: JSOT, 1982); E. Hobsbawm and T. Ranger, *The Invention of Tradition* (Cambridge: Cambridge Univ. Press, 1983). Cf. J. van Seters: "J's use of the stories about the eponymous ancestors is meant to express a strong ethnic identity so important to a people scattered in exilic and diaspora communities. In contrast to Dtr, J expresses this identity in a more universalistic fashion, both temporally and geographically, and as a positive relationship to 'all the families/nations of the earth'" (*In Search of History: Historiography in the Ancient World and the Origins of Biblical History* [New Haven: Yale Univ. Press, 1983] 361).

wives while in the land of the Terahite inheritance suggests the sociohistorical setting of the exile as the context for the shaping of the ancestral stories into their final form.

This conclusion on the redaction of the texts demands that we specify how the three narrative cycles form a unity in this final shaping. Genesis 36–50 explains that the Terahite lineage developed into an extended family when it lived outside the land of its inheritance. Nonetheless, this extended family is connected, in proper genealogical fashion, to the vertical genealogy to whom Yahweh gave the land originally. This genealogical legitimation is accomplished through narratives linked together on the basis of certain subjects: genealogy, marriage, land (here the emphasis on the family burial cave is crucial), and the names of individuals not only in the Terahite lineage, but one removed from it, that is, Ishmael. In these narratives, the ancestors are idealized as people removed from the land, as sojourners outside the land of their ancestors. With the loss of land, genealogy provides status and indicates who is a member of the community. The texts emphasize the necessity of proving one's lineage in order to demonstrate membership in the group.[8]

The above suggestions are grounded in an attempt to reconstruct the history of the formation of Genesis based on an analysis of the biblical literature. In order to be convincing, this tradition-historical argument must be checked against comparable data from outside the Hebrew Bible on how people dispossessed from their land struggle with issues of identity.[9] Does independent evidence exist to bolster my suggestion regarding the context of the final formation of the ancestral stories?

Two biblical scholars interested in identity formation in the exilic and postexilic community have argued for a connection between life outside one's homeland and the importance of establishing one's genealogical tree. D. L. Smith and J. Weinberg examine community organization and social identity among those who returned to the land.[10] Smith's study of the "Fourth World,"

---

8. See Neh 7:61-65 (=Ezra 2:59-63) on those who cannot prove their lineage upon returning from exile. In other words, they are unable to prove that they are true members of the community.

9. Thomas B. Dozeman discussed this point with me in a private conversation.

10. Smith, *Religion of the Landless*. J. Weinberg, "Das Beit 'Avōt im 6.-4. Jh. v.u.Z.," *VT* 23 (1973) 400–14; idem, "Die Agrarverhältnisse in der Bürger-Tempel-

people without their own land, specifically concludes that in the postexilic period notions of the "father's house" widened beyond their usage in earlier times. Moreover, he argues that the ability to demonstrate inclusion within the father's house was a requirement for membership in the postexilic group and established the character of this group.

Smith suggests that the rationale for an expanded understanding of the "family," those included in the Terahite lineage at the time when the kinship group is removed from the land, can be found in what he terms the "social ecology of domination."[11] What Smith understands to be the social structure prior to the exile might be reflected in the ideology of the Sarah-Hagar and Rebekah cycles—as opposed to the Rachel-Leah cycle. When kinship results in inheritance of family land, the lineage designates a single heir to receive this patrimony because a large parcel of land divided among a number of heirs will result in units of land too small to be economically productive. However, horizontal expansion of the lineage—the Rachel-Leah cycle—occurs as "the result of a combination of social crisis and the centralized economic policies of the Chaldean land resettlement and possibly even labor needs."[12] Smith's theory of increase in size of family units in the postexilic period may find support in the stories of Genesis. From what Smith suggests about the social dynamics in the exilic period, as well as what others argue about traditions of origins, we find one possible sociohistorical framework in which the texts fit. The texts become a means to legitimate the group in exile and, when they return, to allow them to exert control over those who remained on the land; those in exile are the true descendants of the Terahite lineage now seen in its horizontal genealogical formation.

Viewed in this way, the Genesis family stories are metaphors for answering the question of who the true Israel is—that is, answering questions of identity, particularly after 587 BCE.[13] The

Gemeinde der Achämenidenzeit," *Wirtschaft und Gesellschaft im alten Vorderasien* (ed. J. Harmatta and G. Komoróczy; Budapest: Akademiai Kiado, 1976) 473–86. For an English summary of Weinberg's argument, see P. E. Dion, "The Civic-and-Temple Community of Persian Period Judaea: Neglected Insights From Eastern Europe," *JNES* 50 (1991) 281–87.

11. Smith, *Religion of the Landless*, 120.

12. Ibid., 118; see also Smith's discussion on 116–20.

13. S. Japhet argues that this is the issue raised by the Golah lists in Ezra-Nehemiah. These lists may be one attempt to answer the question of who is

texts reflect an ideology whereby kinship relationships expressed through genealogies are used as metaphors for understanding the sociopolitical relationships in the postexilic community. The true Israel is a family of brothers who can trace their ancestry back to the vertical patrilineage of Terah. Furthermore, the texts suggest that Israel only became Israel through the circumstances of exile in Egypt, at a time when members of the community lived outside the land. Yet the true Israel can be reckoned only according to strict lineage calculations. Within the exilic community these texts establish who belongs inside the group and who is to remain outside it. The three narrative cycles together provide a means to connect those who were removed from the land (the Rachel-Leah cycle) with those who remained in the land after the Babylonian defeat (the Sarah-Hagar and Rebekah cycles). At the same time this group of texts gives priority to those removed from the land; only in the circumstances of exile did the "true" Israel come into existence. The narratives are intended to shape reality in favor of those removed from the land, rather than to reflect conditions upon their return.

In conclusion, one notes that outside the land Jacob's sons dwell together as equals, just as Terah's sons had done earlier. Life in the land brings fission, but life outside the land becomes the occasion for fusion. Thus, the conclusion of the ancestral stories brings family structure back to its initial starting point of equilibrium—that is, with Israel outside the land of its inheritance.

Israel after the exile; see "People and Land in the Restoration Period," *Das Land Israel in biblischer Zeit* (ed. G. Strecker; Göttingen: Vandenhoeck & Ruprecht, 1983) 112–18.

CHART I: OFFSPRING OF TERAH THROUGH ABRAHAM AND SARAH

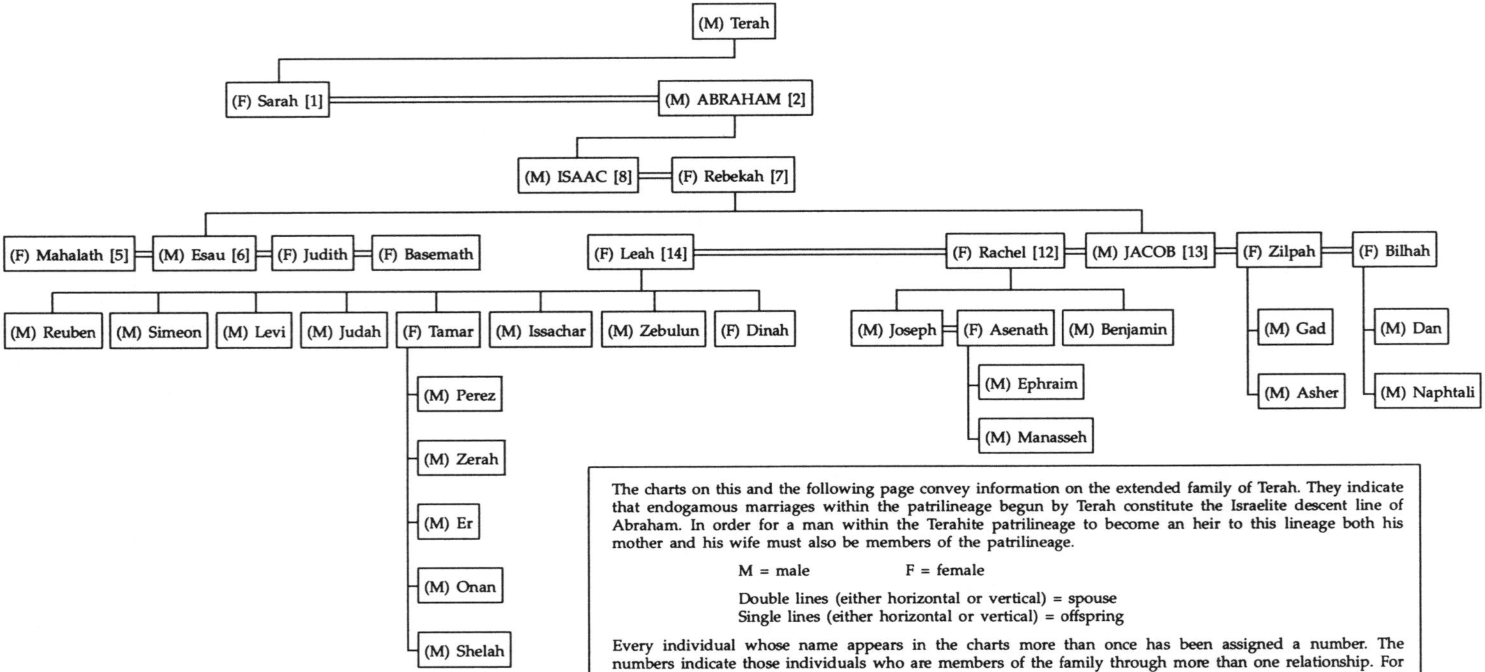

The charts on this and the following page convey information on the extended family of Terah. They indicate that endogamous marriages within the patrilineage begun by Terah constitute the Israelite descent line of Abraham. In order for a man within the Terahite patrilineage to become an heir to this lineage both his mother and his wife must also be members of the patrilineage.

M = male   F = female

Double lines (either horizontal or vertical) = spouse
Single lines (either horizontal or vertical) = offspring

Every individual whose name appears in the charts more than once has been assigned a number. The numbers indicate those individuals who are members of the family through more than one relationship. For example, Rebekah, a female listed as number 7, is a daughter of Bethuel, who is the son of Milcah and Nahor. Rebekah is within the collateral (sibling) patrilineage of Terah. Rebekah marries Isaac (no. 8), who is the son of Abraham (who is a brother of Nahor) and Sarah, who are also within the collateral patrilineage of Terah. The marriage of Isaac to Rebekah establishes Isaac as an Israelite heir to Terah.

CHART II: OFFSPRING OF TERAH THROUGH OTHER UNIONS

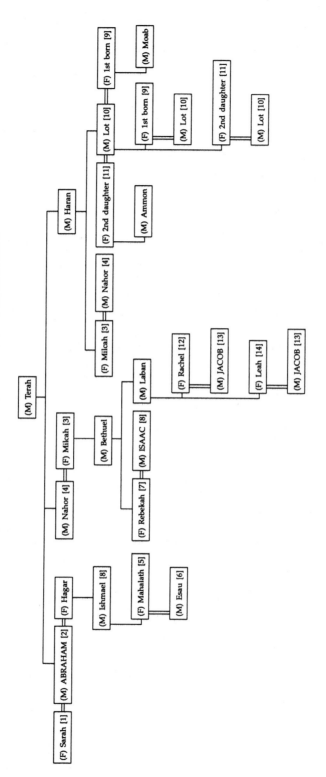

Glossary

Agnate: a relative through the male descent line.

Bêt 'āb **(house of the father):** the household, the smallest basic unit of social organization.

Direct dowry: material goods passed from parents to their daughter upon her marriage.

Endogamy: marriage within boundaries established by an individual's group.

Exogamy: marriage outside boundaries established by an individual's group.

Extended family household: the addition of relatives, either of an elder or younger generation, to the family household.

Family household: a coresidential group comprised of a married couple, any of their unmarried children, and servants. The term may also apply to a widowed individual living with a child or children.

Indirect dowry: gifts given by the groom to the bride.

Multiple-family household: a domestic unit that contains more than one conjugal pair.

Polyandry: a polygamous marriage in which a woman has more than one husband.

Polycoity: a form of marriage in which a man takes other women, who are of lower status than his primary wife, as his secondary wives.

Polygyny: a form of marriage in which a man may have more than one wife at a time, but the women are of equal status.

Serial monogamy: a form of marriage in which an individual may have only one spouse at a time.

Sororal polygyny: a form of polygyny in which a man marries sisters, women of equal status to each other.

Select Bibliography

Abu-Lughod, L. "The Romance of Resistance: Tracing Transformations of Power through Bedouin Women." In *Beyond the Second Sex: New Directions in the Anthropology of Gender*, edited by P. Sanday and R. G. Goodenough, 313–37. Philadelphia: Univ. of Pennsylvania Press, 1990.

———. *Writing Women's Worlds*. Berkeley: Univ. of California Press, 1993.

Coats, G. W. *Genesis with an Introduction to Narrative Literature*. Forms of the Old Testament Literature, vol. 1. Grand Rapids, Mich.: Eerdmans, 1983.

Donaldson, M. E. "Kinship Theory in the Patriarchal Narratives: The Case of the Barren Wife." *JAAR* 49 (1981) 77–87.

Fortes, M. "The Structure of Unilineal Descent Groups." *American Anthropologist* 55 (1953) 17–41.

Goody, J. *The Orient, the Ancient and the Primitive: Systems of Marriage and the Family in the Pre-industrial Societies of Eurasia*. Cambridge: Cambridge Univ. Press, 1990.

———. *Production and Reproduction: A Comparative Study of the Domestic Domain*. Cambridge Studies in Social Anthropology, no. 17. Cambridge: Cambridge Univ. Press, 1976.

Holy, L. *Kinship, Honour and Solidarity: Cousin Marriage in the Middle East*. Themes in Social Anthropology. Manchester: Manchester Univ. Press, 1989.

Lamphere, L. "Strategies, Cooperation, and Conflict among Women in Domestic Groups." In *Woman, Culture, and Society*, edited by M. Z. Rosaldo and L. Lamphere, 97–112. Stanford, Calif.: Stanford Univ. Press, 1974.

Lévi-Strauss, C. *The Elementary Structures of Kinship*. Boston: Beacon, 1969.

Meyers, C. *Discovering Eve: Ancient Israelite Women in Context.* New York: Oxford Univ. Press, 1988.

Oden, R. A. *The Bible without Theology: The Theological Tradition and Alternatives to It.* San Francisco: Harper & Row, 1987.

———. "Jacob as Father, Husband, and Nephew: Kinship Studies and the Patriarchal Narratives." *JBL* 102 (1983) 189–205.

Prewitt, T. J. *The Elusive Covenant: A Structural-Semiotic Reading of Genesis.* Bloomington and Indianapolis: Indiana Univ. Press, 1990.

———. "Kinship Structures and the Genesis Genealogies." *JNES* 40 (1981) 87–98.

Rosaldo, M. Z. "The Use and Abuse of Anthropology: Reflections on Feminism and Cross-Cultural Understanding." *Signs* 5 (1980) 389–417.

Silberman, L. H. "Listening to the Text." *JBL* 102 (1983) 3–26.

Speiser, E. A. *Genesis.* AB. Garden City, N.Y.: Doubleday, 1964.

Steinmetz, D. *From Father to Son: Kinship, Conflict, and Continuity in Genesis.* Louisville: Westminster/John Knox Press, 1991.

Thompson, T. L. *The History of the Patriarchal Narratives: The Quest for the Historical Abraham.* BZAW, no. 133. Berlin: de Gruyter, 1974.

Van Seters, J. *Abraham in History and Tradition.* New Haven: Yale Univ. Press, 1975.

———. *Prologue to History: The Yahwist as Historian in Genesis.* Louisville: Westminster/John Knox Press, 1992.

Vawter, B. *On Genesis: A New Reading.* Garden City, N.Y.: Doubleday, 1977.

Von Rad, G. *Genesis: A Commentary.* Rev. ed. OTL. Philadelphia: Westminster Press, 1972.

Westermann, C. *Genesis 1–11: A Commentary.* Minneapolis: Augsburg, 1984.

———. *Genesis 12–36: A Commentary.* Minneapolis: Augsburg, 1985.

———. *Genesis 37–50: A Commentary.* Minneapolis: Augsburg, 1986.

White, H. C. *Narration and Discourse in the Book of Genesis.* Cambridge: Cambridge Univ. Press, 1991.

Index of Scripture References

Index of Modern Authors